SS Daughter

A Love Story

2nd Edition

Unmasked

by Marlena Berlin
and Gaetano Catelli

Front cover photos: upper right — father in his *Waffen*-SS uniform in Kraków, Poland; upper left — father and I around the time mother left us; bottom — my teen years.

Rear cover photo — father in Lemberg (now Lviv, Ukraine).

Fonts: Plain Germanica and Bookman Old Style.

ISBN: 0692498028
ISBN-13: 978-0692498026

Dedication

To my father, Werner, and my mother, Nina, for doing their best (in spite of their own early trauma); to my sons, Lukas and Johan, whose love gave me the strength and courage to rebuild our lives, and sustained me when hope was very hard to find; and to all the children in the world who, despite great suffering, still believe in love and the goodness of humanity.

Acknowledgments

Special thanks to the office of German World War II military service records, *Deutschen Dienststelle* (WASt); and to author and researcher Thomas Casagrande.

Notes to the 2ⁿᵈ Edition

In the 1ˢᵗ edition, a black rectangle covers the eyes of people in photos. But, while writing the soon to be published "SS Daughter: Book II — Only in America", I said to myself, *No more masks!* And so in this 2ⁿᵈ edition of Book I, although pseudonyms are still used throughout, no one's eyes — including mine — are hidden behind a black mask.

In addition, there have been some cosmetic changes to the text and layout. But the truth of the events described, and their meaning to me, remain unchanged.

Foreword

What follows is a true account of my life, to the best of my recollection. Of course, I cannot remember the exact words I spoke and heard decades ago. And, until I came to America, all the words were in High German (when I was conversing with father) or Austro-Tyrolean dialect (when I was speaking with anyone else in South Tyrol, Italy, which is where I grew up). But the words I've placed in quotation marks capture, as best as I am able to remember, the truth of what was said. My inner thoughts, likewise as best as I can recall them, appear in italics.

Statements about the historical context that shaped my parents, and indirectly me, are based mainly on entries in Wikipedia or on family lore. They are not meant to be a definitive historical account, but rather my subjective understanding of how my upbringing was affected by broader social currents.

Some chapters are arranged chronologically; others are arranged by topic. Inevitably, there is some overlap, and hence a certain amount of repetition is required to ensure clarity.

Because of the sensitive nature of the material, it has taken me a long time to decide to write this memoir. For the sake of discretion, all of the names of people (including mine), places, and things have been changed, except for the names of countries, large cities, public figures, and a few well known consumer items.

My hope is that readers of this book may gain increased confidence that with hard work, and competent and compassionate help, they or their loved ones can overcome even extremely difficult life circumstances.

Namaste,

Marlena Berlin
Queens, New York 2015

Prologue

... I shall die more easily when I have finished writing this story. I have no right to call myself one who knows. I was one who seeks, and I still am. But, I no longer seek in the stars or in books — I'm beginning to hear the teachings of my blood pulsing within me. My story isn't pleasant. It's not sweet and harmonious like invented stories. It tastes of folly and bewilderment, of madness and dreams — like the life of all people who no longer want to lie to themselves. (*Demian*, Hermann Hesse)

I am 5 years old, sitting in the back of my parents' Mercedes sedan, in the spring of 1964. My father, Werner, and my mother, Nina, are shouting at each other, as they often do. I'm leaning forward, trying to absorb what they're yelling, as I often do. But things don't feel typical — they feel dangerous.

Suddenly, mother tells father to stop the car. Elegantly dressed and made up (as always), she exits wearing her camel's hair coat, with an umbrella in one hand and a suitcase in the other. Her high heels tap-tap-tap on the wet pavement of a cold and rainy night in Munich, Germany, as I watch her walk away from her marriage to father and her responsibilities as a mother to me.

She's abandoning me to be raised by father, who spent World War II as a frontline soldier in Adolf Hitler's *Waffen*-SS. Since then, his greatest regret about the war is that Germany lost.

Father is tall, still handsome in middle age, always finely dressed, and possessed of a commanding presence. Plus, he's quite generous with women — myself included. But, he's also a womanizer who quotes from the most misogynistic passages of Schopenhauer and Nietzsche, and cites Hitler, approvingly, as justification for his beliefs and behaviors.

He drinks heavily, and when alone with me is often sexually predatory. He's an absolute tyrant who will brook no dissent, and has a violent and unpredictable temper, resulting in his often assaulting me physically and psychologically.

In my early teens, I become a heroin addict to avoid feeling any more pain.

At age 21, I inherit all of father's properties, which would be worth several million dollars in today's money. But in under 3 years, my inheritance is lost to my heroin habit, and to "friends of the family" who take advantage of my vulnerable condition.

Mother rescues me and my sons in 1983, taking us with her to America. I arrive with a few dollars, 2 small boys, an 8th grade education, and a 1-ounce packet of heroin. With help from mother, and God above, I slowly begin to rebuild my life.

And yet to this day, in spite of the harm he caused, I still love father — the one person in my life who never abandoned me. Since his death, I've spent my life trying to find him again.

Contents

Südtirol

Though Berlin, Germany is where I'm born, I'm raised in Süd-tirol (South Tyrol), a mainly German-dialect speaking region in northernmost Italy that father and his family are from.

While writing this book, I received a letter from Wolfgang, a nephew who still lives in Bolzitano, the South Tyrolean town where I grew up. Besides typical family matters, the letter discusses South Tyrol in the early 20th century. What follows is derived from his letter, plus several articles in Wikipedia.

In 1918, toward the end of World War I, Italy seizes South Tyrol from Austria, because this region is the only part of the southern slope of the Alps that Italy doesn't already control. South Tyrol is formally transferred from Austria to Italy by the Treaty of Versailles in 1919, the year father is born.

At the outset, the government in Rome sensibly allows South Tyroleans a good deal of autonomy in local affairs. For example, because then about 90% of the locals speak a dialect of German, South Tyrol is officially bilingual.

Italianization

In the 1920's and 1930's most of Europe undergoes political-economic upheaval. Amidst the turmoil, Benito Mussolini (like Hitler, a battle-scarred WW I veteran), emerges as Prime Minister of Italy. By 1925, he's turned Italy's then-immature political culture into a 1-party dictatorship. (Like Germany and Japan, Italy wasn't a unified nation til 50 years earlier.)

The belligerently nationalistic Mussolini soon embarks on an aggressive program of Italianizing South Tyrol. All the names of South Tyrol's cities, towns, and villages, as well as all the streets and town squares, are changed from German dialect to Italian. Monuments celebrating Italian culture are erected in every community. Writing or speaking the German language, or its South Tyrolean dialect, is outlawed. People can be arrested and imprisoned if they speak German or dialect in public. When father is a child, the only German-language schools in South Tyrol are secret ones set up with the aid of Michael Gamper, a German-speaking Catholic priest.

Father with staff in one hand, 2 daffodils in the other, and a long feather in his cap. The photo is obviously posed, but scruffy boots and humble surroundings suggest modest circumstances.

In addition, Mussolini creates industrial zones in South Tyrol (which is mainly rural at the time), and relocates factory workers there from regions of Italy farther south — in order to dilute the percentage of German-dialect speakers.

The Italian government also seizes land from many South Tyrolean natives. Mussolini's troops commandeer the large landholdings of my great uncle, Werner (whom father is named after), to use as army barracks.

The forced Italianization of South Tyrol provokes a great deal of anger and unrest among its German-dialect speakers. A number of rebel groups are formed, and there are even some bombings aimed at Mussolini's government.

At the same time, Adolf Hitler's Nazi Party, though not yet in power, is growing in strength in both Germany and Austria. Many German-dialect speaking South Tyroleans are attracted to Nazism because they hope (naively, as it turns out) that Hitler intends to someday unite South Tyrol with Germany, thus relieving them of Mussolini's Italianization program.

When Hitler gains control of Germany in 1933, South Tyroleans are even more hopeful. Hitler's 1938 annexation of Austria, soon followed by his seizure of the German-speaking region of what is now Czechia, further encourages South Tyroleans to believe Hitler will reunite them with the other German and German-dialect speakers of Central Europe.

Pipe Dream

Hitler never seriously intends to annex South Tyrol. The Italian parliament deposes Mussolini in 1943, and surrenders Italy to the US, British, and other Allied forces already advancing from the south. Hitler reacts by seizing control of Italy north of the Allied battle lines, and makes Mussolini his virtual puppet-on-a-string. South Tyrol's German-dialect majority continue to believe Hitler will at last reunite them with their Austrian brethren.

Around this time, Hitler makes a train trip that passes through the area. A lot of South Tyroleans (including a relative who later relates the story to me) wait for him at a station along his route. They want to see Hitler and wave their greetings to him, hoping he will show them some sign of encouragement. But, as Hitler's private train passes through the station, the shades are drawn — he doesn't even bother to look out his window.

3

The fate of the South Tyrolean people doesn't matter to him in the least. Like so many millions of others, they're just pawns in his monstrous criminal scheming.

Stayers vs. Leavers

Father in adolescence, holding a flagpole (instead of a staff). Translation of inscription on back: "March to keep Südtirol German."

A few months before the start of World War II, Hitler and Mussolini enter into a pact called (in English) "The Option". Under its terms, the German-dialect speakers of South Tyrol are to have the choice of resettling in lands recently incorporated into Germany (the Leavers), or remaining in South Tyrol (the Stayers). The Leavers are to have the full rights of other German citizens. The Stayers will lose all claims to autonomous status, and will have to give up all expressions of a Germanic cultural identity.

South Tyroleans don't know if they should leave everything behind, and move to some place in easternmost Germany that few of them have ever seen. They've been promised all kinds of assistance in resettling. But, can they trust Hitler to keep his word? The farmers (a large portion of the population) are especially uncertain. Will a different farm in another locale be as good as the one they'd be leaving behind? And yet, to stay is to risk being arrested and sent to prison for speaking their native language. Though many South Tyroleans don't trust Hitler, they don't trust Mussolini either.

A local political party is urging South Tyroleans to be Leavers. The party's slogan is *Wir gehen nach Hause in das Reich!* (We're going home to the Reich!) Another group is telling people to be Stayers, because one way or another Mussolini and Hitler will someday be out of power, and South Tyroleans can then resume their traditional ways — without interference from Rome *or* Berlin.

The South Tyrolean population is deeply divided by the Option. The Leavers condemn the Stayers as traitors; the Stayers denounce the Leavers as Nazis. The little pharmacy in Bolzitano can't keep enough sleeping pills in stock, because townspeople are having so much trouble falling asleep.

De-Germanization

It turns out that the Leavers have made a disastrous choice. From 1939 until 1943 (by which time it has become clear to most people that Germany and Italy will lose the war), about 75,000 South Tyroleans emigrate to Germany. Only about 50,000 ever return. Pre-war Germany's newest territories in the East, where the Leavers have been relocated because Hitler wants to Germanize these lands, are in the midst of some of the fiercest fighting of World War II.

By the end of the war, Germany has lost these eastern territories, and the non-German local population takes revenge on everyone and everything German. They carry out ethnic cleansing of their Germanic neighbors on a massive scale. Estimates of the number of ethnic Germans who are driven out, or simply flee, run from 12 million to 14 million. The estimated number of Germanic people who die ranges from almost 500,000 who are killed outright, to over 2,000,000 dead due to all causes, including diseases, malnutrition, and exposure to the elements. Many women are raped. Some are crucified after being gang-raped.

Ironically, the Stayers are the ones for whom it is relatively (though not entirely) safe to be Germanic, because during the war Mussolini does not want to antagonize his German allies, and with democracy restored in Italy after the war, South Tyrol regains semi-autonomous status.

But, South Tyrol doesn't completely escape the horrors of the era. Another grim irony is that from 1933 to 1939, the South Tyrolean spa town of Merano is a place of sanctuary for Jews who've fled persecution by Nazis in Germany and Austria. According to political analyst Jonah Goldberg, as long as Mussolini retains power, he refuses to deport, from *any* of the territories he controls, a single Jew to a Nazi death camp (notwithstanding his shameful anti-Semitic 'Race Laws' of 1938).

But, as noted, in 1943 Hitler seizes complete control of Northern Italy. It is then that the ADO (a Nazi-dominated group of local vigilantes) rounds up the Jews of South Tyrol, and either places them in a concentration camp there in Merano, or deports them to a death camp like Auschwitz in Poland. And, scores of Merano's Jews are killed or die of causes related to their captivity while still in Merano.

The Gentiles of South Tyrol face dangers too, though not nearly of the same magnitude. The ADO violently attacks Stayers for not having chosen to fight for Germany. Further, as late as 1945 the ADO tries to force Stayers to enter the war, even though the war has obviously been lost at this point. The ADO also attacks South Tyroleans who are fleeing to the American- and British-controlled areas farther south in Italy. (In spite of all this, none of the leaders of the ADO are ever brought to justice for their crimes.)

It is a scary and dangerous time for the great majority of Europeans, but South Tyrol largely escapes major fighting. For this reason, the caves in its remote mountains prove useful to the Nazis as a hiding place for art works and other valuables stolen from across Europe. When the US Army occupies South Tyrol in May of 1945, it finds vast amounts of looted art treasures and other precious items, including railway wagons filled with gold bars, hundreds of thousands of meters of silk, and scores of works of art stolen from galleries such as the Uffizi in Florence. Hollywood made an all-star movie, *The Monuments Men* (2014), depicting these recovery efforts.

South Tyrol Today

Nowadays, South Tyrol is among the most prosperous regions of the European Union. In spite of Mussolini's Italianization program, and the fact that many thousands of Leavers never returned, plus the globalization of recent decades, more than 60% of the population of South Tyrol still speak German dialect as their 1st language. For native speakers of Italian, the figure remains under 25%.

The Tyrolean Alps in early spring, as seen from the backyard of the home where I grew up (which is still in my family).

𝕿𝖍𝖊 𝕾𝕾

Overview

The SS (*Schutz-Staffel;* literally, security staff) is formed in 1920 as the protection arm of the Nazi Party. In other words, they are Hitler's street fighters for brawling with Communists and other radicals in the civil disorders that plague Germany from the end of World War I (1918) until Hitler comes to power (1933). Once Hitler is in power, the members of the SS continue to swear their allegiance to him, and to him alone, rather than to the German state. Hitler chooses a mousy bureaucrat, Heinrich Himmler, to head the SS and carry out the Holocaust — the cold-blooded execution of approximately 10,000,000 civilians, the majority of whom are Jews.

Waffen-SS

What is extraordinary about both world wars is not that Germany lost them, but that this one nation — with marginal assistance from a few feeble allies — held most of the world at bay for four years between 1914 and 1918, then again for six between 1939 and 1945. I have scarcely met a man who fought against the Germans who did not emerge with a profound respect for their gifts as soldiers, sailors, airmen...especially in 1944-45, when they were hopelessly out-gunned. (British historian Max Hastings)

The war-making arm of the SS is called the *Waffen*-SS (Weaponized SS). Members of the *Waffen*-SS are for the most part frontline soldiers who are especially courageous — and ruthless — in battle. It is estimated that one third of the *Waffen*-SS are killed in combat, due to their fearlessness on both offense and defense. As a rule of thumb, in World War II the number of soldiers in a combat unit who receive a non-lethal wound equals the number who are killed outright.

Father and Uncle Hubert

When World War II breaks out in September 1939, father has

recently turned 20, and his older brother, my uncle Hubert, is a month away from 30. They couldn't have avoided being conscripted into one military or the other. In the Italian Army, they'd have been giving up their cultural identity, and supporting the suppression of their culture in the place of their birth. By fighting for Germany, at least they could speak their native language without getting arrested.

Since I began writing this book, I have come into contact with Thomas Casagrande, an author researching the more than 2,000 South Tyrolean men who joined the SS during World War II. I learn from him the Waffen-SS units father and Uncle Hubert were in. Father was in the *Deutschland* regiment of the *Das Reich* division, and he was one of the 19 South Tyrolean men who were chosen for officer candidates school.

From a photo album of father's. Possibly a training exercise.

Das Reich fights in the Battle of France (1940), Operation Barbarossa (invasion of Russia, 1941), Operation Typhoon (attack on Moscow, 1941), the Battle of Kursk (the largest tank battle ever, 1943), the Normandy landing (the largest invasion by sea ever, 1944), and the Battle of the Bulge (the last German offensive in the West, 1944). It is likely that no division of any country, in Europe or the Pacific, sees fiercer fighting over the whole course of World War II.

Uncle Hubert is in the 6th SS Mountain Division Nord, which spends much of the war fighting the Russians in Kareliya, a region overlapping Finland and Russia. In late 1944, the surviving members of this division are marched 1,000 miles on foot to defend western Germany, which by this time has been invaded by America and its allies. In the final days of the war, what's left of 6th SS Mountain Division Nord is destroyed by the US Army 71st Infantry Division.

Organized Crime

After the Nazis are defeated, the war crimes tribunal conducted in Nuremberg, Germany declares the SS to be a criminal organization. Unlike veterans of Germany's regular armed ser-vices, veterans of the SS receive no benefits (although there were exceptions for those drafted into the SS from foreign countries). Many are jailed, a dozen are executed, many others flee to foreign countries to avoid capture and prosecution. Near the end of his life, father has a reunion with some of those who find sanctuary in South America, as will be discussed in a later chapter.

Based upon the inscriptions on the photos he sends home to his parents during the war, father is in Kraków, Poland and in Lviv (then in Poland, now in Ukraine) sometime during 1944. In both of these cities there are a great many gruesome atrocities committed by both sides, including mass rape and murder of civilians. In Kraków, the grandfather of my American friend Olga is murdered by Germans that same year. Was my father somehow involved with her grandfather's death? We will never know for certain.

According to WASt (an organization that keeps records on 18,000,000 of Germany's World War II service personnel), father is hospitalized twice, both times in Prague (capital of what is now Czech Republic). Since he never mentions to me, or to mother, having been wounded, I assume the hospitalizations are because his childhood hepatitis A had acted up. Whatever the reason for father's hospital stays, during periods of recuperation from illness, soldiers in the *Waffen*-SS are often assigned to guard duty in death camps or other concentration camps. Is father tasked with guarding a camp before returning to the frontline? I don't know.

On back of the photo on page 11, father writes to his parents, "I know what you are thinking. But I am who I am."

Krakau 19.10.44

Regardless of whether father himself sees camp duty, those members of the *Waffen*-SS who do, once back with their combat unit, surely talk about what they witnessed while they were guards. So, contrary to what many of them later claim, members of the *Waffen*-SS could not have been unaware of the horrors being committed in the camps. Whatever the specific details of his involvement, to one degree or another, father is complicit in the crimes committed by the SS.

Unwelcome Home

In general, the Leavers who return to South Tyrol are not warmly received by the Stayers. It is kind of like the Vietnam vets returning to America in the 1970's, but much more so. At least the Vietnam vets did not get America itself destroyed. Whereas, in addition to the massive death and destruction that the Leavers visited upon neighboring countries, they also helped bring disaster and eternal shame upon Italy and Germany. Thus, men like father and uncle Hubert are shunned by their own people.

The uncle Hubert I knew was the kindest man ever, so softspoken and peaceful. But because he was in the *Waffen*-SS, after the war is over the authorities arrest and imprison him in Pisa, Italy for a time. While incarcerated, Hubert is not allowed to have any visitors. Because of the meager food rations, he is a mere 110 pounds when he's released. He returns home to Bolzitano with his spirit completely broken.

Father manages to evade imprisonment after the war. But, he does not escape confinement altogether. In the latter months of the war, he becomes a prisoner of the British. In the prisoner of war camp where he is held, a lack of food causes further damage to his liver.

Hilda

One of the documents I receive from WASt is a copy of father's 1944 application to marry Hilda, his 1st wife. In accordance with Nazi law regarding qualifications for marrying a member of the *Waffen*-SS, Hilda must attest that she's a "pure Aryan", and provide references from others both that she's not a sex worker (who has thus lured a lonely soldier into marriage) and that she has no history of mental illness.

On the front of the photo on page 11, father indicates it is taken in Kraków on October 19, 1944. He clearly has a wedding band on his finger. So by then they've married.

After the war, Hilda hides father from arrest in her Berlin apartment. Unlike the rest of the German military, each soldier in the *Waffen*-SS has his blood-type tattooed under one shoulder, because so many of them are made unconscious by their battle wounds. After the war, this is used by the Allies to identify those who fought in the *Waffen*-SS. However, father already has a scar from a hot liquid having fallen on his back when he was a child. With Hilda's help, he has his SS tattoo removed, and the scar tissue from his childhood scalding obscures traces of the tattoo.

Hilda is about 10 years father's senior and, according to him, she's an alcoholic. Whatever the case, their marriage ends in divorce. His having been divorced, before he marries my future mother, affects how Hubert's wife, my aunt Martha, views me during my childhood, as shall be seen.

Once the war is over, Italy refuses to give father a passport because he was a Leaver. So, he is stateless for a time. But in the 1950's, Germany provides a German passport to SS veterans originally from countries other than Germany, because most of these recruits were forced to serve. Although he volunteered, father nonetheless qualifies to receive a passport, because he is from South Tyrol, not Germany.

I don't know how long father is in hiding, or how he gets back to South Tyrol. But once he returns, he starts a number of businesses, with uncle Hubert as his partner.

Open Wounds

Like many others who fought in World War II, father is a tortured soul for the remainder of his life. He saw (and perhaps participated in) too many horrors during the war to ever have anything but a grim view of the human condition. In today's world we realize that many of those who survive a war, both combatants and civilians, suffer from post-traumatic stress disorder. But, back then, neither group gets any help for it.

The bitter division between Leavers and Stayers continues long after the war is over. I never hear the war discussed in public during my childhood, but in a small town like Bolzitano, the topic hangs over us like a dark cloud. Though my nephew Wolfgang was born in 1969, he feels this tension even today (75 years after the end of the war). Although he meets all of the requirements for membership in the local police force, Wolfgang's employment application is denied anyway. He believes he was rejected because his grandfather, my uncle Hubert, was a Leaver. Even if this is not the actual reason, his feeling this way shows that the tension remains.

As a child, I myself could feel a strange vibe hanging over the town, as if there were lots of secrets that no one would reveal to me. I always felt out-of-place in Bolzitano, like a wrongly knitted sweater. There are several reasons for this, as will be discussed in later chapters. But, I now understand that one of the reasons is that father and uncle Hubert were Leavers. And not just Leavers — they were in the *Waffen*-SS.

This may explain, at least in part, why father does not socialize with most of the other townspeople. In light of the split between Leavers and Stayers, it's not surprising that father largely avoids social get-togethers (except with fellow war veterans).

This silence about South Tyrol's past extends to school. I remember loving history in elementary school, and especially middle school. We are taught a lot about ancient history — Egypt, Greece, and Rome — and about the Middle Ages. However, when it comes to World War II, it is discussed on only 1 occasion, and not in any depth. It is a big taboo — *definitely* a big taboo.

Lebensunwertes Leben

Until receiving Wolfgang's letter, I also didn't know that the Jews of South Tyrol, along with political dissidents and those who have mental or physical disabilities, are rounded up and placed in concentration camps during the period from 1943 on, when Hitler has taken control of Northern Italy. According to Hitler, these groups (as well as Roma, gays, and a number of others) are *Lebensunwertes Leben* (lives unworthy of life). The Wikipedia article states that the Nazis constantly expand the definition of *Lebensunwertes Leben*:

Those considered to be "deviant" or a "source of social turmoil" in Nazi Germany and [Nazi-]occupied Europe fell under this designation. The "deviant" category included the mentally ill, people with disabilities, political dissidents, homosexuals, interracial couples, and criminals. The "social turmoil" category included Communists, Jews, Romani people, Jehovah's Witnesses, "non-white" or non-Caucasian peoples, and some clergy. More than any other of these groups, the Jews soon became the primary focus of this genocidal policy.

The concept culminated in Nazi extermination camps, instituted to systematically kill those who were unworthy to live according to Nazi ideologists. It also justified various human experimentation and eugenics programs, as well as Nazi racial policies.

Development of the concept

According to the author of *Medical Killing and the Psychology of Genocide,* psychiatrist Robert Jay Lifton, the policy went through a number of iterations and modifications:

Of the 5 identifiable steps by which the Nazis carried out the principle of "life unworthy of life," coercive sterilization was the first. There followed the killing of "impaired" children in hospitals; and then the killing of "impaired" adults, mostly collected from mental hospitals, in centers especially equipped with carbon monoxide gas. This project was extended (in the same killing centers) to "impaired" inmates of concentration and extermination camps and, finally, to mass killings in the extermination camps themselves.

So, South Tyroleans have a *great deal* to avoid talking about.

𝕱𝖆𝖙𝖍𝖊𝖗'𝖘 𝕱𝖆𝖒𝖎𝖑𝖞

Father's mother, Astrid, and his father, Hubert, Sr, are natives of South Tyrol. Grandfather Hubert fights for Austria in World War I. As already noted, Austria and Italy are on opposing sides in that conflict, and part of the outcome is that South Tyrol is annexed by Italy.

Grandmother Astrid works as a seamstress. Grandfather Hubert starts out as a blacksmith, but later becomes an auto mechanic, in keeping with the times. They have 2 sons: Hubert, Jr (my uncle Hubert) is their first-born. He's followed almost a decade later by Werner, my father.

Grandfather Hubert is fiery, impulsive, and sometimes almost brutishly insensitive. I've been told that grandmother Astrid would pretend to be busy sewing until late at night to avoid being close to him. (Much later, I adopt a similar pattern in my relationships with men.)

Father is a very handsome boy who is spoiled by his mother, and has the temperament of his father: strong-willed, impulsive, and difficult to handle. Uncle Hubert is the opposite: easy-going, quiet, diplomatic, not always trying to be the center of attention, and an all-around compassionate human being. (Father too is very compassionate oftentimes. The problem is the other times, as shall be seen.)

Uncle Hubert and Aunt Martha
(My Sanctuary, Sort of)

Uncle Hubert and aunt Martha live in an apartment near ours, with a common balcony. When I am very young, father and aunt Martha have an argument so bitter that he never sets foot in their house again. (I'm not sure, but it may have been a dispute over property and money.) They live right across the balcony from us, making the situation that much more awkward. But, by the same token, their apartment is a nearby refuge where I am safe from father's volcanic temper.

To escape from father for awhile, I go there pretty much daily. My aunt and uncle have 6 children. Their youngest, Astrid, is named after our grandmother. She's about 3 years older than me, and I look up to her as a role model. We form a close bond. (After we're grown she betrays me, causing me terrible pain and permanently altering my life. However, my poor cousin's own life turns out tragically, as shall be seen.)

With mother gone, father typically stays out very late. I often wake up scared in the middle of the night because I'm all alone. At times such as these, I climb out of our bedroom window (wearing wool stockings in winter), and go down the stairs in order to avoid the locked gate topped with metal spikes father built to lock me in — and everyone else out. (I often climb over it during the day, but am afraid to do so at night.) Once down in the yard, I walk about 30 feet, then climb another set of stairs, go over to uncle Hubert and aunt Martha's apartment, and knock on their bedroom window. They would then open the window and pull me through.

When father gets home, sometimes as late as 4 or 5 in the morning (drunk by then), he would call them on the telephone, make a huge scene (as if aunt Martha and uncle Hubert are to blame for his leaving me all alone at night), and demand that I be sent home right away. These scenes make me feel that I'm the cause of the trouble.

Uncle Hubert tries to protect me from father's violent temper. One night, I ask him to walk me home, because I'm so afraid of father's anger. Soon the 2 brothers are in the kitchen throwing bottles at each other, arguing over me. It's horrific — I'm afraid they're going to kill each other. I'm conflicted throughout childhood between feelings of guilt and sorrow.

Understandably, aunt Martha isn't happy that I'm in their life. I don't blame her. Besides being at the center of scenes father inflicts on her household, as I grow older I'm hyperactive, I don't listen, and I do things purposely to upset her.

Panty Raid

But then, Martha is mean at times for no reason. For example, she gives chocolates to her own children, but not to me. And, she's quite obvious about it. Or, she might take my dolls and say, "They're *Astrid's*." Worse, Martha would steal my underwear(!) Because mother from time to time sends me American brands of clothing that aren't available locally, I'm certain the underwear is mine. When I discover that Astrid is wearing my underwear, I say to Martha, "This is *my* underwear." She replies, "No...", as she hits me in the mouth with stinky rubber gloves. (Martha wears rubber cleaning gloves around the house until they are so old they are in a state of decay and smell nasty.) I become afraid to say anything, so I don't get my underwear back. But I don't really care. I'll put up with anything just to maintain peace in our family.

When I'm a child, it seems odd to me that Martha saves *everything*. For example, she has whole containers filled with every button she's ever owned. And, when her rubber gloves finally are so worn that they have holes, she cuts them up and makes rubber bands out of them. (Those smelly old rubber gloves!) But as an adult, I realize she'd lived through the severe shortages of World War I, the Great Depression, and World War II. And for a time after WW II, she was raising several children on her own while Hubert was in prison. Having survived years of doing without, she has her reasons for saving even ordinary things for a rainy day.

More Catholic Than the Pope

Martha is very religious. She and Hubert go to church every Sunday, and sometimes I go with them. She'd say things like, "You're not a child of God. You won't go to Heaven, because your parents aren't really married. Your mother is a Protestant, and your father is a divorced Catholic. God doesn't like that." But, to "comfort" me, she'd add, "I'll pray for you, so that you do get into heaven."

Although I've always believed in God, at a young age I decide that organized religions are hypocritical. I see that my aunt is going to church, but I also see how she treats me. In my heart, I know her being mean to me is wrong. And, it's not only aunt Martha — there are plenty of church-going hypocrites in little Bolzitano.

Playmate

Growing up, I'm often very angry (mainly due to father). By age 8 or 9, one way I'm acting out my anger is by reading *Playboy* in front of aunt Martha. Besides being hyperactive, and curious about such things, I know it will drive her crazy.

In Europe at the time, there's no age limit on buying a magazine like *Playboy*. A minor can even buy cigarettes, beer, and wine. I actually don't care that much about these magazines. Father parades around naked in front of me all the time (more on this later), so pictures of naked women aren't a big deal to me. I'd sit at Martha's kitchen table perusing *Playboy*, waiting for her to go berserk. In short order, she'd rip the magazine out of my hands, tear it up, and toss the shredded pages into her wood-burning stove. I'd sit there laughing, because I find it hilarious that Martha gets so worked up. I do this quite a few times just to rile her.

Like the rest of us, Martha is only human and, obviously, I could be a difficult child. When Astrid is born, Martha is already 45. And, she's 48 the year I'm born. So by the time Astrid and I are running about her house screaming and carrying on, as kids often do, Martha is at an age when most people want more peace and quiet, rather than uproar.

Contributing to her worries is memory loss. For example, very day she heats milk on the stove to add to the *ersatz* coffee she makes out of barley, figs, and chicory (another echo of wartime shortages). She serves it with cookies. Her cookies and *ersatz* coffee are the highlight of my afternoon. But she'd often forget the milk until it boils over and makes a mess. She'd then exclaim, "Jesus and Mary, there goes the milk!" The family would laugh. Sadly, her condition gradually worsens. She begins to confuse the names of her own children.

Another burden on Martha is the care and feeding of my grandfather Hubert, Sr, who lives in an adjacent apartment, but takes his meals with Martha and Hubert, Jr. As mentioned, Hubert, Sr, like father, has a volatile temper, which he sometimes takes out on Martha (though he's always nice to me). In his later years, I share with Martha and my cousins responsibility for taking grandfather for his daily walk after dinner, and helping him get ready for bed. Helping in this way allows me to stretch, by about 45 minutes, the amount of time I can avoid going home to father.

I enjoy helping aunt Martha with housework when I visit. Assisting her with chores gives me a sense of belonging to a family. It is still many times safer to be with her than with father. I will always be grateful to Martha for this.

Grandfather Hubert and I at the dinner table.

My Defenders

Uncle Hubert always defends me, whether from father or aunt Martha. Often my aunt and uncle have disagreements over me. For example, she'd whisper something mean about me to him. He'd respond, "You have to be nice to Marlena. She's family. She doesn't have a mother — and her father is *crazy*." So, uncle Hubert is a safe person for me. But, he's afraid of father, and so is everyone else (except Astrid).

Cousin Astrid

Astrid is both beautiful and artistically talented. She's short as a child, but when she turns 13 or 14, she shoots up to 5′ 8″ or 5′ 9″ (I'm 5′ 7″). She weighs 120 pounds (maybe a little less), and has the long legs and gorgeous figure of a model. I think her life is perfect. Back then, I'm unaware that she's suffering greatly on the inside.

I feel safer when Astrid is present, because she's a buffer between father and me. Like uncle Hubert, she always stands up for me. However when I'm 11, Astrid enrolls in an art school in Val Gardena, an Alpine valley that's known for the large colony of artists who live and work there. Her leaving Bolzitano is a big loss for me. My friend, my protector, my virtual big sister has moved away.

Although she's only 14 when she leaves for art school, Astrid and 2 other students rent an apartment together. At the time, I think she's the luckiest girl in the world, because she's escaped from boring Bolzitano and our crazy family.

I still go next door when I have the chance. I'd sit with uncle Hubert, and while he sips his herbal tea, we'd watch television movies together. Westerns set in America are his favorites. Aunt Martha doesn't want us to watch Westerns, because they depict violence. Uncle Hubert would respond, "It's only a movie."

But now that Astrid is gone, I feel sad and lonely. She's my idol. During childhood, and as a young adult, I want to be like her by going to art school too.

What I don't know then is that Astrid will be diagnosed as severely bipolar by the time she's 20 or 21, and that her mental illness will have tragic consequences for her.

𝕸𝖔𝖙𝖍𝖊𝖗'𝖘 𝕱𝖆𝖒𝖎𝖑𝖞

Mother's family are Berliners. My grandmother Frieda is 18 or 19 when she marries grandfather Albert, who is then 25. Mother, their only child, is born a year later, in 1935.

During World War II, Berlin is completely destroyed, first by bombs from the air, then by block-by-block fighting in the streets. (CBS war correspondent Eric Sevareid said the buildings were bombed into ruble, the ruble was bombed to dust, and then the dust was made to bounce.)

Post-war, Berlin is divided between Russia, America, Britain, and France. It's soon the center of international tensions in what comes to be called the Cold War. Having already survived 2 *hot* wars, Frieda's mother, my great grandmother Wilma, moves from Berlin to Munich, Germany. As shall be seen, Wilma's Munich residence will play a part in my life.

Grandfather Albert

Albert's father, Albert, Sr, is a brilliant engineer whose several patents made him wealthy at age 26, and an eventual director of one of Germany's largest industrial conglomerates. Albert's spoiled by his father's wealth, and his mother's indulgence. He doesn't have a strong work ethic, but he does have expensive hobbies like guns, hunting, and women — lots of women. He owns a driving school in Berlin, and has affairs with some of the young women who are his students.

In spite of Albert's privileged background, he and Frieda live in a small 1-bedroom apartment in Berlin. They have parties with smoking, drinking, and playing cards until the early morning hours. After the party, mother is shifted from the bedroom to the living room, which smells of cigarette smoke and stale nicotine. Because of this, mother never smokes.

In my view, Albert and Frieda aren't ideal parents. Both are very self-centered. They have lots of arguments over his infidelities, and there may have been domestic violence. Plus, they're both problem drinkers. When mother is still a child, Frieda divorces Albert on account of his cheating.

War Stories

Albert, Sr, was a teenager during the social and economic chaos that wracks Germany in the years that follow World War I. Like more Germans than is now generally realized (as was discussed on pp. 4-7), he has a foreboding that Hitler will eventually bring ruin to Germany. So, he puts a large portion of the family money into a bank account in The Netherlands, which is a neutral country between the wars and thus (he naively assumes) safe from Hitler.

During World War II, Albert, Jr, is in the *Wehrmacht*, Germany's regular army (not in the *Waffen*-SS like father and uncle Hubert). Albert holds the rank of *Oberleutnant* (1st lieutenant). Based upon his civilian experience as a driving instructor, he's assigned to train recruits to operate military vehicles. As the war progresses, he's variously stationed in France, Poland, Ukraine, and Russia. While in France, he makes a mental note of a town in which the local records office is destroyed by the fighting.

As it turns out, Hitler ignores Dutch neutrality and invades the Netherlands. Luckily, the family's money remains undisturbed in the same bank when Albert, Jr, goes to withdraw it after the war. But, there's a hitch. The Dutch don't want to release any monies to German nationals until they're sure it hasn't been stolen from Jews or other victims of Nazi thievery. And, it's hard to prove a negative.

However, Albert has an idea. He presents himself to the bank officials as a citizen of France whose documents were lost when the records office (mentioned above) was destroyed. The bank believes him and releases the family's money to him.

Albert loves Italy, and decides to start anew there. He and Albert, Sr, cross the Alps into Italy on foot, so as to avoid declaring to customs officials the cash they are carrying.

Albert settles in Milan with a new identity and a new wife. They soon have a son, my uncle Giovanni. Later, Albert marries a 3rd time, and has another daughter. In spite of his family wealth, though, he doesn't provide for any of his 3 children once he's divorced from their mother. (Frieda also marries twice more, but mother remains her only child.)

Albert spends lots of leisure time traveling between Germany, Austria, and Italy. Reputedly a good marksman, he collects rifles and handguns, and goes to shooting competitions in all 3 countries. He makes lots of friends, including many women friends. He also writes stories and poems, a number of the latter about his affairs with women.

Father and grandfather Albert in front of Albert's trailer.

In his last years, Albert travels around Italy with a trailer hitched to his Porsche sports car, accompanied by Uta, the new woman in his life. They spend their summers in our backyard in Bolzitano, connected to our electricity, and using our water when they shower. In this way, they don't have to pay for utilities. They spend their winters in Sicily. (I don't know what arrangements they make there for electricity and water.)

Albert lives a basically carefree life. As already mentioned, he does not support any of his 3 children, or even worry about them. And yet many people love him, and he has friends everywhere. He's a born comedian who is great at telling jokes, and he seems to know 100's of them. There is a German word for such a person: *Lebenkünstler,* a master at the art of living. Although I didn't get to know him well, I have fond memories of Albert.

Grandmother Frieda

Unlike Albert, Frieda and her twin sister, Beatrix, don't have a happy childhood. Wilma's husband is a strict father (though not so strict with himself). For example, the children have to show him their homework every night, no matter what. Even if he comes home from a bar at 1 or 2 AM, he still awakens them — and their 3 sisters from his previous marriage. The 5 girls would have to show their homework to him in the middle of the night. If something isn't to his liking, he beats them. Needless to say, they're terrified of him.

Perhaps because of their abusive father, Frieda and Beatrix don't have warm personalities. Frieda, especially, is emotionally cold. Beatrix is a little bit warmer, but not by much. I think they have a big part in influencing mother to leave me behind when she separates from father.

In the early 1950's, Frieda moves to Canada to join Beatrix, who has already settled there with her husband, Gregor. When Frieda leaves, mother is 16 or 17, and not yet out of high school. During this period, mother lives with Frieda's mother, Wilma, who is a very sweet woman.

Love and Marriage

While in Canada, Frieda marries her second husband, Wasily, and thus obtains Canadian citizenship. Wasily dies from cancer in the late 1960's or early 70's. Frieda then contacts her former husband, my grandfather Albert, to explore the possibility of remarriage. She voyages to France on an ocean liner for a romantic rendezvous with him.

But once on board, she meets Austin, a fine gentleman from Australia. Austin is quite wealthy — he owns 2 radio stations in Sydney — and they fall in love mid-passage. When the ship arrives in France, Albert is waiting at the dock with roses. Frieda informs him, "I'm sorry, Albert, I've met Austin, and I'm going to marry him and move to Sydney."

The Crazy Twins

When I'm still a child, Beatrix and Frieda (before Frieda's move to Australia), while both are drunk, might phone me from Canada — although it's the middle of the night in Italy.

If father is home when they call, he'd be 1st to wake up and answer the phone. He can't stand Frieda and Beatrix to begin with, because he blames them for talking mother into leaving him. (When mother 1st left, she stayed with them in Canada, before settling in America.) He'd shout at them, and sometimes hang up the phone without giving it to me. Unafraid of him, because they're safely an ocean away, they'd call right back — relishing the fact that they're upsetting him! He'd relent and hand me the phone, angrily referring to them as *die verrückten Zwilinge* (the crazy twins). Once I'm on the phone, they'd take turns speaking. Frieda would promise me the world — along with new clothes and a new bedroom set — none of which ever happens.

Fashion Fixation

Frieda and Beatrix always look elegant. Both are invariably well-dressed, wearing fine jewelry, with their nails and hair done just so. Mother seems to have inherited their fixation on appearing perfectly turned out. She loves to go shopping, and she looks beautiful all the time, as if she has stepped out of the pages of Vogue.

Like Albert, mother can be sweet and funny, in her case almost childlike. But, she can also be angry and impulsive, like father. She is never completely independent financially, so she remains somewhat at the beck and call of the much better off Frieda, which Frieda takes advantage of. For instance, though Frieda at times telephones when it is midnight where mother is living, mother would stay on the phone with her.

Left to right: Beatrix, Frieda, mother, and me.

She never says to Frieda, "Could you please call earlier?" Or, "I'm tired, mother; could you call tomorrow?" No matter how exhausted, mother would stay on the phone, because Frieda is so demanding — and might stop giving her money.

Frieda's Way

By 1973, though I'm not yet 15, father can't handle me anymore. I have a serious drug problem, and I'm basically out of control (details to come). So, father sends me to the US to live with mother. Near the end of the year, mother takes me and Kim (my newborn sister by mother's 2nd husband) to Sydney to visit Frieda. We stay there for 3 months. Frieda's husband, Austin, turns out to be a lovely man.

Frieda can be quite funny after she's had a few drinks (which is often). I remember getting drunk with her that New Year's Eve. Earlier in the evening, she does Tarot card readings to entertain us. After everyone else has gone to bed, Frieda and I keep drinking. The 2 of us are getting really drunk and having a ball dancing together, while she sings Frank Sinatra's hit, *My Way*. At the end of the night, Frieda is too drunk to walk. Fortunately, she is a small woman — a mere 4' 8" or 4' 9" — so I'm able to carry her up the stairs to her bedroom without much difficulty.

Austin dies sometime in the mid-1980's. Frieda, now independently wealthy, leaves Sydney and moves back to Seattle, where Beatrix still lives. At first, Frieda lives close by Beatrix. Later, they live under the same roof, until Frieda dies in 2005, about age 90.

After mother dies in 1994, Frieda essentially disowns Kim and me, apparently because at the funeral we ask Frieda to not make any disparaging remarks about mother or either of our fathers. Soon after, Frieda cuts off all contact with us.

Aunt Beatrix

In her late 30's, Beatrix marries Gregor, an aeronautical engineer who's a bit younger than she is. Immediately after World War II, it's difficult for an engineer to find work in Germany, because most of German industry was destroyed during the war. But Gregor is able to find a job in Montreal, Canada, working for Boeing. And so Beatrix and Gregor relocate there in the 1950's. Later, Gregor is transferred to the Boeing headquarters in Seattle, Washington, where they spend the rest of their days.

Gregor drinks a lot of whiskey, and he's mean to Beatrix. He's also very biased: He hates liberals, Asians, and Blacks, among others. (Gregor hates a lot.) Though they're childless and their marriage is not especially happy, Beatrix and Gregor stay together till the end.

In 1973, due to an economic downturn in the US, Gregor is laid off by Boeing. As a result, Beatrix moves from Seattle to Munich to live in Wilma's old apartment. (Although Wilma has died, the family has kept her apartment.)

Gregor plans to soon join her, because by the 1970's German industry has been largely rebuilt. Indeed, by then the country is experiencing a labor shortage. (Germany had lost about 10% of its population in the war.)

But unexpectedly, he's called back to work by Boeing, so Beatrix returns to Seattle. However, luckily for me, she happens to still be in Munich when I'm arrested there for drug possession. In cooperation with my parents, she bails me out of jail, and then puts me on a flight to Arlington, Virginia to live with mother. (Details to come.)

Gregor retires from Boeing, after working there for 30 years. As mentioned, Frieda moves to Seattle to be with them after her last husband, Austin, dies. Gregor gets a decent pension from Boeing, and the 3 of them continue to live together in Seattle during their final years.

Beatrix and Gregor later claim they notified Kim and me, via telegram, of Frieda's death in 2005. But Beatrix and Gregor are around age 90 themselves, so their memory may have been faulty. In any case, I didn't receive such a telegram, and neither did Kim. So, we don't attend Frieda's funeral.

In 2007, when Gregor dies, Kim and I do attend his funeral. It's the saddest funeral I've ever been to, because at that point all of his friends have passed away. So, besides Kim and myself, there's no one in attendance but Beatrix. By now, she's unable to manage on her own. Kim and I sell her apartment and its furnishings, and move her into an assisted living facility.

Beatrix dies in 2008, at age 93. Frieda's will left her inheritance from Austin to the childless Beatrix, who leaves what remains of that to Kim and me. Ironically, though Frieda does not intend for us to inherit Austin's money, in the end we each get a portion of it. Kim and I decide to give part of our inheritance to Gregor's nephew, because he'd have been an heir of Gregor if Beatrix had died first.

𝕎hen 𝕎erner 𝕄et ℕina

Werner, my brooding father, is born in August 1919. Nina, my light-hearted mother, is born in March 1935. As mentioned mother is in some ways the opposite of father, very sweet and funny — almost childlike. But, much like father, she's also quite impulsive. Their complementary temperaments, combined with a nearly 16-year age difference, will make for great romantic passion, but also result in explosive conflicts.

As noted, mother's parents, Albert and Frieda, divorce when mother is still a child. Frieda then moves to Canada, but mother, who's still in her teens, moves to Munich to live with her grandmother Wilma, Frieda's mother.

In general, Albert is an absent father for all 3 of his children. But he has a life-long romance with Italy, and every year he takes mother with him to Merano. Notwithstanding its dark chapter when Hitler reigned (see p.6), Merano is a gem of a little city, not far from Bolzitano. Surrounded by the Alps and dotted with palm trees, it has an almost tropical climate.

A building father owns in Bolzitano has a gas station and a restaurant as tenants. Albert and mother always stop there for fuel and food on their way from Munich to Merano. (Father's other properties include several condominium apartments, a small bed-and-breakfast, a mechanics' garage, and a farm equipment manufacturing business.)

Nina meets Werner on one of these trips. (This may have been Albert's intention.) Father is handsome, charming, always well-dressed in a hand-tailored suit, mature (when he's on his best behavior), and a financially stable business owner — all of which mother likes. They begin to date. He's very generous, and gives her beautiful presents, which of course she also likes. Mother feels protected by him, financially and otherwise.

They marry in 1957, and I'm born in September of the following year.

Page 31: Nina and her father, Albert. Page 32: Werner, 1956 or 1957.

Sturm und Drang
(Stormy Weather)

But, father has another side. Later, mother would say, "He's like a natural catastrophe." We never know when a storm will strike. They seem to come from nowhere — but suddenly we are in the middle of one of his hurricanes.

My parents on their wedding day.

I believe mother senses this before she marries him. Yet, at the time she's in her early 20's, and doesn't know what to do with her life. Frieda is in Canada, and aside from the annual trips to Merano, Albert isn't in the picture. She's a little lost and Werner, besides being a charming father-figure with his own businesses and real estate interests, owns a home with a spacious backyard and a large swimming pool. That part all looks good. But, though mother may have already sensed that father has a darker side, she does not foresee her culture shock in moving from large cosmopolitan cities like Berlin and Munich to Bolzitano, a rural hamlet of some 3,000 people.

To be frank, mother is father's trophy wife. Being a wealthy older man's shiny prize can be alienating to other women, especially in a small mountain town. After moving to Bolzitano, mother soon realizes the local matrons do not accept her. She's elegant and sophisticated, and dresses in the fashion of a large city. This isn't their style.

Mother feels the townswomen are always watching and judging her. They look at her from their window when she passes by. When she shops, they stare and seem to be wondering: *What is she putting in her shopping cart? Is she cooking healthy meals? Does she even* know *how to cook?* Mother, who's quite sensitive to begin with, always feels criticized and unwelcome in Bolzitano, and this contributes to the instability of her marriage to father.

Adding to her insecurities, father harshly criticizes mother's cooking, and sometimes eats instead at his still-doting mother's house. It gets to a point where mother says to him, "Why should I bother to cook? Go eat with your mother!"

A Very Difficult Man

As noted, father is a loving and generous man — except when he's being an angry tyrant. If my parents have a major argument in the morning, father might scream at mother, "If you're not packed and out of this house by noon, I'll send my workers to kick you out!"

Day or night, whenever they have a big argument, mother would flee to Wilma's apartment in Munich, a 4-hour drive from Bolzitano, with me sitting in the back of the car. This drama unfolds relatively often.

Whether immediately afterward, or hours later, father would be seized by grief and regret because he's so miserable without us. He'd then drive to Munich, and upon arrival at Wilma's, he'd start shouting mother's name and mine from the street below (at any hour of the day or night), thereby disturbing Wilma's neighbors as well as upsetting mother and Wilma. Before too long, father, mother, and I would all travel back to South Tyrol.

This becomes a pattern: He makes her leave, but then gets her to return; then she leaves on her own initiative, he gets her back; repeat. Lots of fighting, yelling, arguing (mother would throw shoes at him). Even before I am born, one night they have a big fight, and she spends the night in a hotel. He follows her, and they make up. Mother later tells me that I'm probably the result of their lovemaking that night.

Mother and I in late 1958.

Their relationship continues to be turbulent and volatile to the end. Though they legally divorce when I am 3, they don't actually separate until I'm 5. Even so, mother returns to him several times in subsequent years.

A Rainy Night in Munich

By 1964, mother cannot take it anymore (and neither can Wilma). She knows Munich isn't far enough away to escape from father's gravitational pull. She's been in regular contact with Frieda and Beatrix, and for some time they've been urging mother to leave him for good. They say of father, *"er hat einen Jagdschein,"* which literally means "he has a hunting license", but is slang for *he's a crazy stalker.* The 3 of them plan for her escape.

I remember crying in the back seat of our car on that rainy spring night in Munich, when she walks away from her responsibilities as a wife to father, and as a mother to me. Her walking away frightens me, and I wonder, *Where is she going? Is she ever coming back?*

Because I'm crying, father shouts at me, "Don't be like your mother — don't be hysterical! *All* women are hysterical! Women are simply *crazy!"*

As usual, I'm terrified and don't want to do anything that will upset him anymore than he already is. Whenever father gets angry while driving, he goes wild and speeds like a demon. In subsequent years, there are times when he pulls over to the side of the road and says, "You know, I should drive off the cliff [or hill or mountain — wherever we happen to be] and kill both of us." So, it's always better to remain perfectly quiet. While father seethes with anger, I sit in silence on the ride back from Munich that night.

Years later, I ask mother why she didn't take me with her. She answers that at the time she asked me to choose: Did I want to stay with father, who has a large yard with a fruit orchard and a big swimming pool, and with whom I could travel and go skiing? Or, did I want to go with her, though she'll be poor, unemployed, and she doesn't yet know where we'd be living. According to her, I chose to stay with father. (However, I do not remember this conversation.)

In fairness to mother, I must add that though the divorce court awarded her legal custody over me, as a practical matter father wouldn't allow her (or anyone else) to take me from him. He's a law unto himself — which is an element of both his charm and his menace.

I don't see mother again for 3 or 4 years.

Life With Father

After mother leaves, the locals feel sorry for father. He's a single dad, which is quite unusual for that time and place. And, he's raising a young daughter — not even a son. Plus, he has many vexing business responsibilities.

What the townspeople are unaware of (or they pretend to be) is that because of father's violent temper, he often assaults me physically and psychologically. He also often behaves in ways that are sexually predatory.

Because father is like a natural catastrophe (mother's metaphor is apt), I never know where or when he'll erupt. If he's having one of his fits, even his workers steer clear of him to avoid getting caught in the whirlwind. But, I *can't* step away. I'm still a child. Where would I go? He doesn't allow me to leave him, in part because he's so emotionally dependent on me (especially with mother gone), and in part because people who are persistently abusive and have impulse-control issues often need an audience. (Tellingly, they rarely act out while they're alone.)

Reign of Terror

As one example of his acting out, father would throw things, chairs for instance, or whatever else happens to be in his path. I remember shaking many times, silently hoping he'll soon calm down, or trying to calm him myself. After awhile he does settle down, but these tantrums occur regularly. If not on one day, then on the next, there is some kind of uproar. It could happen in a public place; it could happen at home with just me there; it could be with his workers. Sometimes his workers would warn me, "Be careful, your father is in a bad mood." And, I'd think, *You're telling* me? *I'm the one who knows him best.*

Rage Radar

I learn to deal with father's fits by developing a special "rage radar", in order to anticipate his next outburst. Whenever I hear him come up the stairs to our apartment, I'm in fear — *Oh, God, here he comes. What kind of mood is he in?*

He might arrive in a good mood and be quite nice. Or, he might show up miserable and angry — so angry that it would be best for me to crawl under a rock. Indeed, I often wish I could be invisible. But, because I don't have my own room (I have to sleep in the same bed with him; more on this later), there's no escaping father and his tantrums when I'm home.

Throughout childhood, I feel utterly helpless, unable to speak up for myself, or to push back in any way. If I disagree with father, or if I voice any opinion of my own at all, he might erupt like a volcano. (Or, he might not.)

I have to be very cautious as to when to approach him, when to remain silent, and when to converse. For instance, he insists that I sit with him while he eats. But, he can sense that I'm not happy sitting with him, and sometimes *this* makes him angry. So, I try hard to pretend to be happy, and I get increasingly good at it (a skill I will often employ later in life).

The outside weather greatly affects father's 'inner weather'. He hates wind, heat, and humidity. When I get a little older, I learn to make note of the weather when he's on his way up the stairs. For example, if it's windy outside, he'll be in a dangerous mood when he gets inside — in which case I'll run and hide in the bathroom.

For the most part, no one helps me get through this. Uncle Hubert tries, but he cannot do that much and, as mentioned, aunt Martha is afraid of father.

SS Charisma

Despite his unpredictable temper, people are strongly drawn to father. As noted in the Prologue, he has a commanding presence: tall, handsome, and always finely dressed. And he's generous to a fault, especially with women. Whenever he enters a room, people stop and stare. Everywhere he goes, people look at him with respect. Women, in particular, are attracted to him; he, in turn, is a womanizer. Father has a strong work ethic, and he's a natural-born leader. His business interests, at their height, employ about 50 people in little Bolzitano. His workers want to work hard and do a good job for him, whether because they fear him, or because they respect him. (Probably a bit of both.)

Father on a tractor he manufactures under license from Porsche.

Although he might have a glass of wine at lunch, he mainly drinks at night, especially on weekends. Drunk or sober, he's always torn by the conflict between his better angels and his inner demons. There's a German expression for this: *von der Tarantel gestochen* (stung by the tarantula). He drinks to relax, but he can't, which is why he drinks too much.

Always the Center of Attention

Temperamentally, we're complete opposites. I greatly admire father's strength, and his not caring what others think of him. But I get upset when he creates a scene at home or in public. I'm the quiet type (like uncle Hubert), so I find father's scenes both frightening and embarrassing.

He needs my admiration and pampering all the time. (I didn't need pampering then, and I don't need it now). At an early age, I learn to often say things I don't really mean (not just at mealtimes) in order to keep father calm.

Most of all, unlike father I don't want to be the center of attention. And yet, being "Werner's daughter" means *always* being the center of attention. Besides father's commanding presence, and his general reputation, we stand out in public because he has no wife, and I have no mother — it's always just the 2 of us. Even when we go to out-of-town places, we're still like a magnet that draws other people's stares.

SS Princess

To this day, I have extremely conflicted feelings about father. I did receive a lot of abuse from him. But on the other hand, being an SS "Princess", so to speak, can be fun and exciting. Father is quite charming when he's in the mood to be.

Until brought low by illness at the end of his life, father always has an aura of SS authority. He has such a powerful vibe that no one wants to arouse his anger. So, it feels like no harm can ever come to me as long as I am at his side.

As mentioned, father is quite generous, and would bring me unusual things, for instance a toy cable car, like the ones we ride in when we go skiing. He hangs it from one wall to another in the kitchen. I have a lot of fun transporting my dolls back and forth on it.

He also buys me a set of Märklin toy trains (a high quality German brand), and at times we enjoy playing with them together on a large table with miniature bridges and tunnels.

As his princess, father takes me shopping at the most expensive stores. In Italy, with enough money, you can buy the world's finest hand-made clothing and leather accessories. On a single shopping trip, he's likely to purchase several pairs of handcrafted Italian shoes for me. Or, several nice dresses or handbags.

Further, I can sign for things I want at the local shops. Not only for food and other household items. Whatever I want, my every purchase is always covered by father.

At age 11 or 12, I'm drinking with father. (In Europe, kids are typically allowed a beer, or glass of wine, or wine with seltzer water.) At an even earlier age, I get to have champagne with him on New Year's Eve. Usually, father and I spend New Year's Eve in a grand pre-war hotel (appointed with walnut-wood paneling, elaborate chandeliers, *etc.*) in the resort town of Sulden, where he's built a 2nd home.

When we travel, we stay at luxury hotels, and we dine in expensive restaurants. *Everything* father does is big and expensive. It's all part of being special because I'm "Werner's daughter". He feels, and he wants me to feel, that we're upper-class sophisticates. Indeed, father *is* special, compared with other men in Bolzitano. In turn, he treats me as if I am special, unlike how other parents treat their children.

In a sense we *are* celebrities, at least by the standards of a small town. Our lifestyle is more glamorous than theirs. Sadly for mother, it's because of our specialness that she's shunned in Bolzitano. Father, by contrast, doesn't care that he isn't accepted by the locals (which, as noted, is something I admire about him).

It's fun to have a father who takes me out of the socially prescribed routine that children with 2 parents typically must conform to. Society doesn't impose its template on him; he creates his own template.

For instance, every winter he takes me out of school to go skiing with him. The school calendar isn't allowed to interfere with his plans. I don't like the attention that results. When I'd get back, kids would ask, "Where were you?" I'd answer, "I went on vacation." They'd follow up, "Why did you go on vacation when there is *school?*" Going on a ski trip while school is in session seems weird to them. This makes me feel awkward, different, out of place. I enjoy these privileges, yet I also feel like I'm a bad person for having them.

So, I like that I can pretty much do as I please. If I want to eat chocolate pudding for breakfast, vanilla pudding for lunch, and rice pudding for dinner, I can. (I make *lots* of pudding!) I grow up feeling alright about being special on that level: It's okay to think outside the box, to cross boundaries, to not follow *all* the rules. I'm grateful to father for giving me that.

However, I also have to endure father's reign of terror. I think this is why, as an adult, I've often been attracted to dangerous men, and the feeling that they're providing me with safety and protection (except from *them*).

City Lights

Because his parents were simple rural folk, the importance father places on feeling he is a worldly sophisticate might be a compensation mechanism. I'm not sure where and when he acquires his expensive tastes. As with many young men from a rustic background, it may be that his first exposure to the refinements of the wider world comes about when he goes off to war. As far as I know, he hadn't ventured outside of South Tyrol before he joined the military.

I think father's eyes are really opened for the first time when he gets to Berlin. Before it is destroyed by the war, Berlin has a lot of cultural ferment — art, theater, music, literature, nightclubs — the kind of ambiance that father wasn't exposed to while growing up in provincial South Tyrol.

Hochdeutsch

Perhaps insecurity about his rustic background is the reason he insists we speak only *Hochdeutsch* (High German) to each other. No one else I know in Bolzitano speaks *Hochdeutsch*; they all speak either the local dialect or Italian. In fact, father himself speaks in dialect with everyone else, just like I do. But when speaking with him, I must speak *Hochdeutsch*.

Also, below the surface, he may feel hurt because Leavers are shunned rather than welcomed back after the war. Perhaps speaking High German with me is a way of distancing himself from the local people, because they've rejected him.

But for me, switching between High German and local dialect makes me feel even more awkward. It's doubly dislocating: We live in Italy, yet speak Tyrolean dialect in public. We live in South Tyrol, but speak High German in private. I really hate it. I don't want to be *different*. I want to speak *Tyrolean* dialect, not *Hochdeutsch*. When local people overhear us, it's one more reason I feel attention is focused on me. Attention that makes me feel like an oddball, like an outsider.

Fragmentation

To survive, I have to split myself. This splitting is sometimes called *fragmentation*. It often occurs in people who are chronically traumatized. I have to make my life 'okay' in my mind, to keep telling myself: *Living with father is a good choice. It's better than living with mother would be.* (I never wish I were living with mother — never once. I always feel that it's better living with father, and just putting up with all the bad stuff.

But, I have to give up my own sense of self to get the benefits of being his daughter. I have to always try to please him. It's *all* about him; I exist to serve his wants. As a child, I never learn what *my* needs are: Who I am, what I want in life, what my positive attributes are — I have no idea. We never have a nice, quiet breakfast, lunch, or dinner.

Summer *Kamp*

I have bronchitis as a child. So, that 1st summer after mother has left, father takes me to Kurhaus Prasura Arosa, a Swiss sanatorium for children. I think father does this to buy time to figure out how he can manage as a single father while running several businesses.

Prasura Arosa presents itself as a summer camp, but it's actually a medical facility for children with bronchial problems. Its location high in the Swiss Alps, where the air is so clean, makes it easier for the kids' lungs to heal themselves.

I sleep on a cot in a large room with other girls. I remember feeling so out of place. I'm not yet 6 years old, mother has up and walked out of our life, and father has dropped me off in this so-called summer camp. It all feels strange to me. I wonder to myself, *Why am I here? What's happening to me?*

Fortunately, I meet Juliette there. She's from Belgium and a little bit older than me. We become good friends, and she helps me feel a little less lost.

Father visits once or twice, and treats us both to an outing. I enjoy his taking us on a cable car ride in the Swiss Alps. But, I am embarrassed to be with him, because he's so big and overpowering. As discussed, he constantly demands to be the center of attention, and I feel so small in his presence.

Always Feeling Different

The Bolzitano of my youth is all-white, almost all Catholic, and predictably traditional in its social attitudes. As already mentioned, our family definitely does not fit the mold, and this draws people's attention to us from the start. As things have turned out, I've been the center of attention my whole life. I've resisted this, because it makes me so uncomfortable. I've always wished I could wear an "invisibility hat".

Among my differences from the other kids is the fact that father is still a Nazi at heart (to be honest about it), and the local Stayers have not forgotten that the Nazis brought complete disaster to much of Europe, including Italy and Austria.

And, mother has roots in 2 cosmopolitan cities, Berlin and Munich. From the outset she's viewed by the locals as somehow "foreign". Nowadays, South Tyrolean homes are as modern as New York's. Almost everyone in Bolzitano has cable television, cellphone(s), a laptop, and an internet connection — whatever technology we have here in America, they have there. But, when mother arrives in the 1950's, South Tyrolean women are still cooking on wood-burning stoves!

She has bleached-blonde hair she wears in a stylish updo. Most women in Bolzitano have undyed hair worn in a bun. Many wear a scarf over their head (as a display of modesty, not as a fashion statement). Mother dresses in sexy skirts and high heels; the local matrons walk about in old-fashioned aprons. Father loves that she's so much more fashionable than the other women. But, father's obvious appreciation of her doesn't increase mother's popularity with them.

Further, mother is a Protestant and, as noted, my parents have married in a civil ceremony, because father is divorced from Hilda. Divorce itself, especially in this nearly all Catholic community, is unusual at the time. And, after mother divorces him, father becomes twice divorced. I remember being perhaps the only child in my elementary school (there is at most 1 other) who comes from a broken home.

Moreover, I look different from the other girls. Most of the other schoolgirls have long hair in braids — like in old movies set in Switzerland. But father (himself) cuts my hair short.

Mother in our backyard in Bolzitano.

Because of my short hair, father's workers call me "Fritz" (a nickname I have to this day). In addition, he teaches me a lot of "boy things". For example, when I'm 9 he insists I drive the tractor he manufactures. (Some boy-stuff is useful to know, so there are good things I learn from father.)

Like him, I break ground for things that become the norm later on. The other girls wear dresses. I'm the 1st to wear jeans. And, they're more advanced than those of Europe's big cities. In the 1960's, jeans made for women in Europe have a zipper on the side. But mother, who's in the US by then, is sending me girls jeans made in America. They have a zipper *in front* (like the lederhosen I wore as a young child).

Because of my boyish haircut and pants, a few times when I walk home from school, 4 or 5 boys would hold hands to form a chain, blocking me from getting past. They'd laugh and make fun of me, saying things like, "She's wearing *boys* pants!" I'd get scared and start crying, and then the bullies would let me through. In retrospect, it all seems silly. But, it's an example of how rigidly gendered things are at the time.

Also, back then relatively few South Tyroleans have their own car. By contrast, father always has the latest motor vehicles. For example, he has an amphibious car that could be driven into a body of water — where it would function like a boat — and then driven back onto dry land again.

Father with one of my cousins and her Alsatian, early 1950's.

He paves the way for others, which is one of the reasons he's exciting to be with. Novel cars, beautiful women, expensive hand-tailored suits — father too is an interesting subject to watch, especially in a small town, where people have an eye out for anything the least bit out of the ordinary. With 2 parents who are each, in their way, a local sensation, I guess it is inevitable that attention is focused on me also.

Lunch

At the time, school children go home for lunch. (Most Italian mothers don't work outside the home, especially in rural areas.) But, in my case father would pick me up at school, and we'd go to a restaurant (another thing making me different).

Often he'd be stressed, because he's responsible for 40-50 employees who depend on him for their livelihood. I'd eat the same things almost every day: rice and gravy, plus lettuce with milk and sugar. I might also have a little bit of veal.

Evening and Weekend Dining

When we dine out in the evening or during the weekend, father always drinks a lot. Before long, 2 or 3 of his friends might join us. So, the meal isn't just an hour; we'd be there for hours on end. I'm bored sitting there watching him and his friends get drunk. So, father would send me to the kitchen, saying, "Go learn how to cook." I get to know all of the chefs in the several restaurants that we regularly go to. However, on occasions when we are at a new place, I don't want to go into the kitchen. I'm still a child, and I'm shy with strangers to begin with. What am I supposed to do, stand there and say, *Hey, guys, teach me how to cook!* If I balk at going to the kitchen, father would say, "Well, have another ice cream." I might wind up having 3, 4, or 5!

Life is Good When I'm With Max

When I'm 6, we're given a boxer by Karla, one of father's girl-friends. Like mother, Karla is tall, blonde, German, and wears her hair in an updo. (He won't date South Tyrolean women.) We name the dog *Max* (after the German boxer Max Schmeling). I love Max, and so does father. Max is definitely a member of our family. Father treats him very well — he's never mean to *Max*. On some nights, father might stay out until 3 or 4 in the morning. I'd enjoy watching television with Max (in Bolzitano we receive only 2 stations, both Italian language), while eating a whole bowl of vanilla pudding as my dinner. At such times, life seems pretty good.

Understudies for Mother

I'm relieved whenever father has a steady girlfriend. I wish he'd remarry, and perhaps have more children, so that his attention wouldn't be focused solely on me. But, he'd say things like, "I never remarried because of *you*," claiming *I'd* be upset by another woman (which isn't so). When he makes such statements, I'd think, *Here we go again — he's blaming me.* (But, I don't dare contradict him.)

I think the real reason he doesn't remarry is that he can't

handle commitment. Aside from mother, he isn't faithful to any woman. I remember one night, around 10 or 11 o'clock, overhearing him drunkenly talking on the phone to a woman friend. He's telling her how much he loves her, trying to get her to come over. Even though I'm still a kid at the time, I think to myself, *What a liar!*

There were times I'd say to a girlfriend of father something like, "Don't think he loves just you." Or, "Someone else will come along, and before you know it, you'll be gone."

Max with one of father's girlfriends (*not* Karla).

Karla, who gave us Max, would at times try to walk me home from school. But, Astrid and I would ride by on our bicycles pretending not to notice her. Karla is trying to 'play mother' to me, but I'm not having any of it.

Housekeeping for Father

Because father is in charge, even the everyday routine of running the household is filled with drama. For the most part, I have to do all the laundering, ironing, cleaning, and cooking (including for the bed-and-breakfast, when school is not in session). Father realizes this is too much for me to do all by myself. So, from time to time he hires a housekeeper, who might help out once or twice a week.

But, every housekeeper soon winds up leaving. Either he fires her, or she quits, because he'd start arguments with her. She might leave in a huff, or she might quietly disappear and never return. No one can stand doing housework for him for long. Then the whole burden reverts to me: all the cooking, cleaning, laundering, and ironing — at age 8 or 9.

Father has at least 40 dress shirts, and they all have to be ironed perfectly. It takes me about 15 minutes to iron the collar for each shirt precisely so. While I'm struggling with his 40 shirts, he might come home, look at the hamper, and ask, "Where's my pink and white-striped shirt?"

If I answer, "I don't know; I've been ironing all these other shirts", he might pick up the hamper and fling it at me from the other end of the hallway. Here comes the hamper, flying in my direction — I have to duck! I'm crying and pleading, "Please don't throw things at me; please don't hit me."

He keeps gaining weight since he eats and drinks too much, including late at night. If a shirt doesn't fit because a button is too tight, he'd rip the shirt into pieces. I'd stand there shaking with fear, thinking *Omigod, he's on a rampage again!*

Strangely, father cuts slits on the top of all of his socks. He insists that tight socks cut off circulation — and in life everything possible must be done to aid good circulation! So, all his socks have 2 or 3 slits cut in them. I remember mother's reaction on one of her visits. She sees that all his socks have slits, and asks, "Why is he doing this?!" (He wasn't doing this before she left.)

I reply, "He's doing it for his circulation." Mother already knows that father is nutty, so she does not inquire further. We both just laugh.

Cooking For Father

Father tells me what to cook for dinner, and I do the best I can. But often, he comes home from work in a stormy mood, lifts the lid off the pot, looks at the contents, slams down the lid, and says something like, "Who can eat this *shit?*" (repeating his behavior with mother).

National Socialist Nutrition

As noted earlier, near the end of WW II, father is taken prisoner by the British. His captors probably don't have enough food for themselves, much less for German POW's. Although there are wild mushrooms growing on the camp grounds, father warns his fellow prisoners not to eat them. But some prisoners are so hungry that they eat the mushrooms anyway. They wind up dying from food poisoning, according to father.

During his confinement as a POW, the hepatitis A that he contracted as a youth flares up again. For the remainder of his life, he's focused on health (though not enough to reduce his excessive eating and drinking).

He often talks about *Hitler's* ideas on healthy living. According to father, Hitler knew exactly what is healthy. Consistent with National Socialist principles, father believes in natural living and eating organic food. He'd say things like, "Be *natural!* Women must be natural. Remember, love finds its way through the stomach. If you want a good man, you need to know how to cook."

As with clothing, father requires that we have food of the highest quality. So, we *must* be organic. We get goat milk, goat butter, and organic meats from farmers in the mountains. We get organic bacon from organic pigs. Father would get a whole pot full of organic honey, and we would have to eat it with some of the bee's wax still in it (which I find kind of disgusting).

Sometimes we eat only buckwheat, because he'd insist buckwheat is the cure for all ailments. At other times, we *have to* eat cranberries daily. Father would come home with 50 pounds of organic cranberries from the mountains, and then I would have to make jam, jelly, and syrup.

So, here we go — another huge job. It is *very important* to wash and clean the cranberries the *exact* way father wants it done. I have to take a white sheet and hang it over a chair, put a bucket under the sheet, and then roll the cranberries over the sheet so the dirt and leaves stick to it.

If I make one mistake with these stupid cranberries, father might throw them all over the kitchen. So, this is a big, demanding project. I'd make at least 20 large jars of cranberry jam, I'd make 20 bottles of syrup too, all of which I'd then store in the cellar. (Father would beam with pride that *his* cellar is well-stocked.) When his food fixation changes to apricots, I'd have to make apricot kompot and apricot desserts. Same with red and black currants. Elderberries too!

How the Party Parties

Although father does have some sensible ideas about what's healthy to eat, he overdoes *everything*. As mentioned, he drinks too much and he eats too much — sometimes eating in the wee hours of the morning. Nothing is ever done in moderation; it is always one extreme or the other. For example, on some weekends he has parties at our house with 10 to 15 of his friends (the ones mother says are all Nazis). Because of all the noise they make, I can't fall asleep until the party winds down. When I wake up in the morning, a number of partiers are passed out on the floor in the living room, or sleeping on the sofa or the guest bed.

Backyard Eden

Or, I can play in our backyard, which is a saving grace. Ours is huge, with lots of trees. It's incredible — every sort of fruit grows in our backyard: cherries, peaches, blueberries, mulberries, strawberries, red currants, black currants, elderberries, walnuts, table nuts, chestnuts, peaches, plums, apricots, at least 4 different types of apples, and 3 or 4 different types of pears. So, there are lots of trees for me to climb, which is what I do pretty much every day. Climbing trees is calming and soothing for me, especially one particular old apple tree.

There's also the swimming pool. I'm in the water much of the summer. When the pool ices over in winter, I skate on it.

Winter Ski Trips

As mentioned, every winter father takes me out of school for a week to 10 days, and we go skiing together. He'd rationalize what is actually selfishness on his part by saying things like, "Look, when you're 21, you'll know just as much. It won't matter that you missed a week of school now. Teachers are 'idiots' [or 'Communists'], and you don't learn much from them anyway. So, we're going skiing." Or, "Just because kids in school have no winter break, parents shouldn't suffer and not be able to go on vacation."

When we travel, the 2 of us sleep in the same room and share a double bed, like at home. This arrangement is the norm until I'm a teen.

Father tries to teach me how to ski, but in doing so he constantly shouts at me. It soon gets to the point where I prefer to teach myself. From the start, I spend as little time as possible on the ski slope with him. When I get a little older, I always ski on my own.

Page 53: Our backyard in Bolzitano in recent years (now owned by a cousin of mine). Page 54: Father and I on a skiing trip.

Summers at the Spa

In the summer we visit Chianciano Terme, father's favorite place in Tuscany. It's a spa that he believes helps relieve the damage to his liver from hepatitis and his excessive drinking.

Set among gentle Tuscan hills, Chianciano Terme has lovely marble fountains surrounded by manicured gardens. But, it's a boring place for a child, because most people there are older. Fortunately, Astrid sometimes comes with us.

The mineral water there has high concentrations of sulfur, so it tastes awful. Of course, father forces me to drink it. In retrospect, I realize he wants me to be healthy. But with father, nothing can ever be fun; everything is always *forced*.

Mother comes with us once or twice. I like it when she's with us, because then I don't have to sleep in the same bed with father. It's kind of strange. Even though she's remarried, when she visits us she sleeps in father's bed.

Though mother loves summer in general, she too dislikes Chianciano Terme. She'd rather be at the beach, lying on a blanket in a pretty bikini. Father suffers in heat, so he hates the beach. He always wants to go to Chianciano Terme or the mountains (another source of conflict between them).

When I'm 10 or 11, the 3 of us are on a car trip to Chianciano Terme. As usual, it's a nightmare. My parents are arguing almost continuously, and mother often cries. She stays only 2 or 3 days. Father then has to drive her to the airport. Once at the airport, mother cries some more. It's not possible for them to spend even a few days together and have a nice time. At such moments I ask myself, *Why does she come? It makes no sense. Knowing how he is, why come at all?*

So, these are our summer vacations. I beg father to send me to summer camp instead. Though I have Astrid to play with at home, I want to be away from father, with a whole group of kids at the beach for 4 to 6 weeks — summer camp stuff.

But, he won't allow it. He says camp isn't good for a child. Actually, he just wants me to always be with him. I run the household, and make sure he's okay. He needs me so much I can never get away. No matter how hard I try, I can't escape.

Though landlocked, Chianciano Terme surrounds its swimming pool with beach sand. I'm frowning because of the silly pose he makes me strike. Note that we are wearing matching swim trunks.

Childhood Friends

For the most part, local parents don't allow their children to play at my house — another way in which I'm different from the other kids. Their parents worry because there's no adult woman in our household — and father does not have the best reputation in town. I do have friends who come to our house to play with me. But, they're not from Bolzitano. They're mainly from Germany, and have parents who are staying at father's bed-and-breakfast. (During the summer months, I have to set out their breakfast and clean their rooms too.)

Astrid is one of my few local playmates. But, instead of climbing trees like me, she prefers playing with her dolls, and walking them in a doll's carriage. I'm not maternal with my dolls. I poke in their eyes, paint their faces crazy colors, and cut their hair off. (Clearly, I'm an angry child!)

There's also my friend Margit (whom father photographed in the nude with me). And, there's Lenora and her brother, Laurenz. They visit me with their mother, Claudia, 3 or 4 times each year, including a week at Easter time and a week in summer. Oddly, Claudia's husband, Klaus, doesn't join her. (I think that Claudia and father are having an affair.)

Her visits are good times for me, because she gets along well with father. She knows how to calm him down, so he's in a much better mood when she's with us. And, because she'd cook, I wouldn't have that to worry about.

For 2 or 3 years in a row, Claudia invites me to Nuremberg, where she and Klaus have a nice house. I'd spend nearly 2 weeks there. These too are good times for me.

But, Klaus isn't very nice to Claudia. One time when he's yelling at her, I confront him, "I thought I got away from father, but you're acting just as crazy as he does!" I have the courage to say this to Klaus, but I'd never have dared say something like that to father. If I had, I'd have gotten a pretty bad beating. Father doesn't beat me every day. His abuse is usually in the form of verbal and emotional outbursts (eg, "You look like vomited barley soup!). Although there is physical violence also, it's not as frequent.

National Socialist Ranting and Raving

In my early childhood, father doesn't say much about World War II. But when I become rebellious in my teen years, he'd say things like, "You should have been in *Russia* — then you'd understand how *hard* life is!" As an example, he tells me about driving a truck in the Russian wintertime. Seeing a civilian woman who's walking in the snow with a bundle in her arms, he gives her a lift. The bundle turns out to be the corpse of her baby, who has frozen to death.

As noted, father has read works by Nietzsche, Tolstoy, and Schopenhauer. Of course, he has also read Hitler's autobiography, *Mein Kampf*. Although father himself is quite opinionated, according to him I don't have a right to opinions of my own. If I dare to express an opinion, he shouts things like, "You shouldn't be *thinking*. Women have *nothing* in their brains. *Horses* have bigger brains!" Or, "Let horses think, because women *can't* think". He attributes to Nietzsche the saying, "Don't forget the whip when you go to see a woman." In other words, women need to be whipped.

Father remains a vociferous anti-Semite to the end. There's a dentist who is one of the few Jews in the entire area (as far as I'm aware), and he isn't even located in our town — he's a half-hour's drive away. It happens that one of my cousins goes to him for dental care. Father's reaction is, "How could she go there? How could she go to a *Jewish* dentist?! Why would anyone ever go to a Jewish dentist? There are other dentists to go to. He's overpriced; he charges more. It's never enough for Jews — everything is always more expensive!"

In childhood I'm already aware of the Nazi-hunter Simon Wiesenthal, because father would curse aloud at any mention of his name. After meals, father would sit in his favorite chair in the living room, and listen to the news on the radio. Our radio is one of those gigantic Grundig models, with 2 large knobs, 1 for the volume and 1 to tune-in the station. (It's so large that it looks like a commode.)

I'd think father is napping while the radio is on. But whenever there is a news report about Simon Wiesenthal (or Israel), father would suddenly start swearing and yelling things like, "The world will find out what troublemakers they are. They're going to cause problems again and again!"

In June 1967, Israel is engaged in a brief war with some of its Arab neighbors (sometimes called "The Six-Day War). Israel is spectacularly successful — and father is absolutely livid. He shouts things like, "Jews are the enemy of all people!"

But then, father says similar things about anyone non-white, or a Communist, or who has ideas different from his own. For example, he gets all riled up over the Beatles(!) According to him, the world is going to hell because of the Communists — and the Beatles. It isn't every day that he says such things but, then again, it isn't unusual.

It's a little atypical that our dog, Max, is a boxer. One thinks of German shepherds as the favorite dog of Nazis. And, indeed, father always says German shepherds are the best dogs in the world, a man's best friend, and so forth. When he's depressed, he'd praise dogs to the heavens. I would think to myself: *Well, why don't you live with just Max — and leave me alone? Then I would have some peace.*

These are a few bits and pieces of his outbursts that I recall. None of it has ever made sense to me. I have never understood why there is such anger and hatred in the world.

Looking back, it seems clear to me that the war permanently damaged father psychologically. I think he had post traumatic stress disorder. He simply couldn't help himself; there was no way he could keep his emotions from flaring up (which is why mother left us, as he himself must have realized).

"We'll Always Be Alone"

Sometime that same year, 1967, father tells me (looking as if he's just learned of a death in our family) "Your mother has remarried. Now she's never coming back to us. We'll always be alone." He still loves her, and has been hoping she'd return. He's completely crushed by this turn of events.

But back then, I feel that I don't care. (As an adult, I've come to realize otherwise.) As noted, mother left when I was 5. Ever since, I've been dealing with life on my own, trying to make everything work — without any help from her. America seems far away, as does mother and her life there. At times I think to myself: *I don't have such a bad life. Other children have to ask their mother's permission to do anything, but I don't.*

Further, I manage to do all the shopping on my own, as well as all the housework. I buy all the food and household goods, from toothpaste to toilet paper to dog food to milk and eggs —

whatever food and sundries are needed, I'm the one who has to buy them. Yet, by the same token, I can get all the foods I enjoy eating — mainly sweet things like fruits and yogurt, and of course, puddings. Sometimes I buy rice, but I almost never buy meat for myself.

So, I figure I'm doing alright without a mother in the house.

Mother, not long before her 2nd marriage.

Organ Lessons

Father makes me take lessons on one of those electronic organs for the home that come out in the late 1960's. I'd rather take piano lessons at the music school in town, because I jump at any opportunity to get away from the house. Father won't allow this; I must have private lessons at home. For my music teacher, he hires Artur, a little man with fat hands and a gold ring on his pinky finger. He's a bit odd-looking, with fringes of hair on the side of his head combed up-and-over to cover the baldness on top.

Private piano and organ lessons are Artur's secondary source of income. His main occupation is working as a hair dresser. When he arrives at our house, his hands are different colors: black, brown, or reddish orange, depending on what color dye he has massaged into a woman's hair that day. Though Artur doesn't do anything bad to me, I feel uncomfortable sitting next to him. Father doesn't understand this (or ignores it), so he arranges for weekly lessons with Artur. I become oppositional — a lot of times I don't open the front door when Artur rings the doorbell!

Father makes me practice every day. He dictates which songs I play, while he sits and listens. I don't want to practice on that stupid organ. It feels so forced that I'm often practicing with tears in my eyes. I want to be playing piano in a music class, where I will be with other kids. I feel trapped and isolated — like *Rapunzel* in her tower (my favorite fairy tale).

Escapism

Prior to my teen years, my main means of escape are cooking, baking, swimming, and climbing trees in the backyard. Also whenever I like, I can go to the local knitting store, and pick out whatever wool I want. By the age of 9 or 10, I'm knitting my own sweaters.

Because I read a lot, the local bookstore is another sanctuary. It sells school supplies too, like Staples combined with Barnes and Noble, though on a smaller scale. I really like going there about once a week and buying new books.

I love the Pippi Longstocking stories. She's my idol — oh, to be like Pippi Longstocking! Her father lives somewhere in the South Seas, and visits her only once every 6 months. He's a nice guy, who brings her a horse and a monkey! Pippi is very strong, so she can beat the stuffing out of anyone who bothers her. I feel helpless as a child. I'm not allowed to have a voice of my own. In my fantasies, I want to be like Pippi Longstocking — and kick ass!

So I read, knit, and make the food I want (all of which father unstintingly pays for). But though I'm by myself much of the time, father is in and out of the picture every day. When he's away from the house, it's peaceful; but, when he comes home, things get dangerous. A lot of the time I feel sad and helpless that this is the life I'm living.

As described earlier, our backyard has lots of trees for me to climb as another escape. I like climbing trees so much that I want to join a circus. With Astrid's help, I hang ropes between 2 trees and try to balance myself on the ropes. (nb: Astrid is not *just* a girlie-girl, and I'm not *just* a tomboy.)

Father has a carpentry shop, as part of his agricultural vehicle manufacturing business. The carpenter, Konrad, is an older man who drinks a bit too much, and is missing a finger or 2 on each of his hands, because of the dangers of his craft. Whenever I want something made of wood, I go to the carpentry shop and ask Konrad to make it for me. To further my dream of joining a circus, I ask him to craft a set of stilts for Astrid and myself. The next day, the stilts are ready, and the 2 of us have a lot of fun walking on them.

Since sports are super fun for me, father builds a swing, gymnastic rings, and a double bar in our backyard. He does *many* good things, for which I'll always be grateful. To repeat, it's because the good and the bad in father are so intermixed that to this day I am very conflicted in my feelings for him.

In summer, I'm often in our swimming pool. I put chairs in the pool and try to use them as boats. At age 6, I'm already entering swimming competitions. Cousin Thorvald is my swimming coach. He's a good coach, and he encourages me. Oddly, father never comes to my competitions. This is unexpected, since he otherwise wants to be with me all the time.

I win some 40 or 50 medals, which I still have. Being a strong swimmer, and part of a team, helps my self-esteem. These too are good times.

As noted, in winter father and I go skiing. I become a pretty good skier. I always want Astrid or my friend Lenora to come with us, so that I won't be alone with father. Likewise, when we go to the beach in the summer, I try to bring Astrid with us, so it won't be just father and me.

St. Nick and *Krampus*

In much of Middle Europe, St. Nicholas's Day is celebrated on December 6. The night before is *Krampusnacht*. A Krampus is a hairy monster that probably originated in pre-Christian pagan legend.

In many Alpine towns on the evening of December 5, a number of men don Krampus costumes. Accompanied by someone dressed as St. Nick, they parade through the streets. (Because of the rowdiness that often results from drinking, the authorities have often tried to suppress or discourage these parades.) It's a little like good-cop/bad-cop: The children are told that if they're good, St. Nicholas will give them presents. If they're bad, a Krampus monster will punish them.

There's an annual Krampus parade in Bolzitano. During my childhood, I'd watch it with father every year. Although I am very afraid of the Krampus monsters, because father is at my side I feel safe and protected.

Weeks before Christmas, aunt Martha starts baking cookies and fruitcake with dried fruit and nuts. This involves a lot of work, and I help her for hours on end. But, all of this preparation is fun for me because it gives me a sense of belonging to a family.

Weihnachten

When *Weihnachten* (Holy Night", *ie*, Christmas Eve) rolls around, people erect a real tree in their living room, with real candles. Early in the day, children are not allowed in the living room. They are told some intriguing story about why they have to be elsewhere — so it is very exciting for them. Meanwhile, adults secretly decorate the tree.

Sometimes a ladder is left outside, beneath an open window, so that the children will think *das Christkind* (the Christ child) has used the ladder to climb in and out of the house.

Martha has a record album that contains traditional German Christmas songs and stories. Astrid and I get to listen to it every day. These are special times. Martha is often very strict, but she can also be very kind.

Page 64: Fanciful depiction of a Krampus monster

Father Christmas

In spite of his often being so difficult, father too can be very endearing. For example, at Christmas time he buys lots of beautiful presents, not only for me but for all 6 of my cousins, and even for Hubert and Martha.

This is confusing for my aunt and uncle, because father can't abide Martha and her religiosity. As noted, he has not set foot in their home ever since he had a big argument with her many years earlier. And yet, when father sees Hubert and Martha together, they never know if he will greet them with an obscene version of *drop dead*, and brusquely walk off; or, say *hello* and smile warmly.

Regardless, father buys expensive presents for Hubert and Martha for Christmas (yet still refuses to enter their home).

But then, father is not stingy at any time of the year. As discussed, when it comes to shopping for me, he doesn't buy only 1 pair of handmade leather shoes; he buys 3-5 pairs. Or, 3-5 fine dresses. In terms of material things — clothes, toys, *etc.* — he gives me much more than I need.

He's even *more* generous with me at Christmastime. And, he's generous with presents and bonuses for all of his workers too! But, father's generosity with me causes awkwardness when I visit my cousins. I am father's only child, whereas Hubert and Martha have 6 children to buy presents for. Naturally, I get more presents than any of my 6 cousins do. I can always sense some envy in the air when I visit them at Christmas, and this makes me feel guilty. I also feel awkward because of father refusing to visit them, as well as mother having left us. Adding to my unease, aunt Martha would express her resentment by saying something petty like, "See how he's spoiling her!"

Uncle Hubert would then speak up for me, "Don't start. Leave her alone — she doesn't have a mother."

No matter where I go, I have to be careful about what I say and do. At home, father could go crazy with anger. At aunt Martha's, she might make cutting remarks out of envy. Or, articles of my clothing might disappear, and she would say they belong to *her* children. There is no real safety *anywhere*.

Father and I at Christmas.

Stille Nacht

On Christmas Eve, it's even more apparent than usual that father has been a lonely and unhappy man ever since mother left. His friends are with their own families, so he has only Max and me to keep him company. Every year, he has me play *Stille Nacht* (Silent Night) on the organ. While I'm playing, he says sad things like, "It's only you and me and Max. The world is such a harsh place. When you grow up, you'll see how difficult life is."

Naturally, I don't want to spend a gloomy Christmas Eve with a sad and lonely man — who at any moment may become very angry. (He can be melancholy one minute, and explode into crazed fury the next.) But, I have to comfort him by saying things like, "It's okay, Papi, you have me and Max, and we love you. Don't worry, it's okay."

Yet I really want to go to aunt Martha and uncle Hubert's. They have 6 kids, and their Christmas Eve celebration is joyous, not melancholy. They sing carols by their Christmas tree. It's always beautiful to see and hear.

But because I feel sorry for father, I feel guilty about wanting to leave him. On the other hand, he keeps repeating himself about the *sadness* of it all, how sad *all* of life is. How the 3 of us are alone in the world (as noted, he always includes Max). Meanwhile, I'm thinking to myself, *When is a good moment to escape from this? When to ask him, "May I please go to aunt Martha and uncle Hubert's?"*

I have to muster up all my courage, because I never know if he's going to have a big fit as a result of my asking. It's agonizing to have to control my every word in order to avoid his blowing up. When I do ask, "May I please go to aunt Martha's?", he might reply, "Sure" — he could be quite nice about it — or, he might have a screaming fit. If he goes off the deep end, I'd quickly say, "No, no, it's okay — I don't have to go. I'll stay with you and Max. It's fine; I'm sorry I asked. I know it's Christmas — I'll stay with you."

Father might then say, "No, just go, just go." Although he'd still be angry and hurt, I'd run out the door, down into our yard, and back up the stairs to Hubert and Martha's home — where I'd feel (almost) safe. After I leave, he'd sulk, feeling so rejected. Yet, he'd just sit there with Max — he won't set foot in their home, because of his enmity toward Martha.

Unfortunately, Martha always seems to feel, *Oh, here she comes.* She doesn't really want me there. But, at least I feel relatively safe — there are more people, so the attention isn't solely on me. In sum, much of the time it's an un-Merry Christmas Eve.

Mixed Signals

Father wants me to appear sophisticated in public. He buys me beautiful hats, gloves, and expensive designer pocketbooks. And yet, he'd say things like, "Women should be natural and not wear makeup. If you want to get a man and keep him, just be natural" (however, always also be eye-catching).

It's all so confusing.

As mentioned earlier, he doesn't respect Bolzitano's school-teachers. In fact, he despises *all* teachers. He calls them "know-it-alls", and yet "numbskulls". One time, when he asks me what I want to be when I grow up, I make the mistake of replying *a teacher*. He loses it and roars, "Why on earth would you want to be a teacher? Don't you know teachers are complete idiots?" He would go on and on shouting insults, and trashing all the world's teachers. I learn to not say again that I want to be a teacher!

But, he gets this way about any profession I mention. When I say to him I might like to be a nurse, he goes bonkers, calls nursing a "dog-ass profession", and asks, "Why would you want to clean up sick peoples' stinking mess?"

If I say, "Whatever you think is best for me, Papi", he would yell, "Can't you think for yourself?!" There is no winning, *ever.* In my imagination, I so wish I were an orphan. In an orphan-age, at least there would be other kids — and I wouldn't have to deal with parents.

Immer Angst
(Constant Fear)

I'm always apprehensive when I get home in the evening, be-cause I never know if I'll find father there. If he's out on the town, I can stay up until 11 — eating pudding and watching TV with Max — and then go to bed and fall asleep.

Father might show up at 2, 3, 4 in the morning — whenever. I'd lie in bed as still as possible, pretending he hasn't awak-ened me. I don't know if he's going to have a good night's sleep, or if he's going to toss and turn. He sometimes makes groaning noises, as if he's in pain.

Mostly, I feel fear whenever father is present. Not mere fear, but *terror.* I shake a lot of the time. I freeze up, because I don't know what to say or do that will avoid a blow-up. But if I don't say anything, if I shut down, he gets *more* upset.

Many times when we're having breakfast, he'd try to talk to me. He may have yelled at me a few minutes before, so I'm afraid to say anything. He might then go crazy, pounding his fist on the table, sometimes yanking away the table cloth, sending dishes and coffee cups tumbling onto the floor. (As always, I have to clean up the mess he's made.)

It's frustrating because, in the heat of the moment, he has no understanding of why I shut down. He's one of those individuals who often doesn't realize how his behavior is affecting other people. A few times, I say to him, "I'm really scared of you." Omigod! I either get a beating, or he screams, "Why would you ever be scared of *me!*"

I'd answer, "Because you're 'going off' and having a tantrum. This is why I'm scared of you." I think he can't admit it, see it, hear it, confront it, or handle it — at least until the storm blows over, and then he drinks to forget.

And so, I stop talking altogether — except to say what I think father wants me to say. It is not who I *am*, or what I *feel*, or what I *want*. I learn to behave in ways that I think will minimize the chances he will get angry. Life with father requires continuous anger prevention and damage control.

I feel constant fear and humiliation. When I'm sleeping, he's there in my dreams — nightmares actually. This goes on for many years. Even after he dies, I have nightmares about him for more than 10 years. (From age 26 until I'm 40, I'm in psychotherapy working on the trauma of my upbringing.)

What father really needs is an *adult* woman who gives him lots of attention. But, his romantic relationships never last very long. So, I'm the one who has to cope with his emotional ups and downs.

The Fall

As mentioned, Father has built a large 2nd home in Sulden, a South Tyrolean village more than a mile above sea level. He loves Sulden, but I mainly dread going there, because on most visits it's only father and me (plus Max). Even getting there is an exercise in tedium, because we always stop at 1 or 2 bars along the way. So, the journey takes hours, instead of what should be less than 45 minutes. But if my friend Lenora, her brother Laurenz, and their mother, Claudia, come with us, I feel better. At least I have added company — and father's focus is not solely on me.

One of the things we do in Sulden is hike in the woods looking for chanterelle mushrooms. Many people consider them a great delicacy. And, chanterelles contain antioxidants, such as beta carotene. This increases their appeal to father.

When Claudia and her children come with us, Father and Claudia would drink wine at one of the local restaurants, while Lenora, Laurenz, and I would enjoy our cake and ice cream. On one trip, we kids are outside playing when it's lightly raining. While we're running about, I climb onto a nearby porch, then slip on the wet surface and fall off.

I feel a bad pain in my right wrist, but I don't tell father, because I'm afraid he'll beat me. A short while later, all 5 of us go hiking in the surrounding woods for an hour or 2. I'm 8 or 9, silently holding my arm as we walk along.

After a bit, Claudia notices I'm in pain. She asks me what's wrong, and I tell her, "I've fallen off a porch, but please don't tell father." Realizing that my pain is intense, not merely a minor discomfort, she does tell father. But I still don't say anything to him, because I'm so afraid he's going to have a major fit and beat me, or at least scream bloody murder.

It turns out my wrist is broken, and I have to be taken to a hospital. These kinds of incidents happen a number of times — I get hurt, but I'm too afraid to tell father anything. I learn to handle my own affairs, and suffer through certain things, not saying anything to anybody.

Red Snow

Another time, I'm on a ski slope with a pair of skis father has given me for my 10th Christmas. Since the skis are new, turning is a bit difficult, and it takes me a little longer. On one downhill run I fall, and while I'm still lying in the snow, a woman skis over my leg. I have a huge cut, blood is gushing everywhere, and the snow around me has turned red. I pull my sock over the wound, thinking I'll get up, continue skiing downhill, and everything will be fine. But, I soon realize I'm bleeding too heavily for that.

Luckily, a ski instructor arrives who knows that I'm "Werner's daughter". He removes my skis, pulls me up onto his shoulders, and skis down the slope with me hanging onto him. He tells me that he has to call father. I scream and cry, "No, please don't call my father, please don't tell him!"

He responds, "We must call your father, because you have to go to a hospital." Though well-intentioned, he doesn't understand that I have been repeatedly abused by father.

I'm very scared when he makes the call. Naturally, father comes (he never fails to show up for me). Although he does yell at me, he also takes me to a hospital. My leg isn't broken, but there is a large wound. I need 30 stitches, and I spend a few days in the hospital while my leg stabilizes.

Summing up: Though I'm always afraid to tell father that I've gotten hurt, at times the injuries are too severe to hide. But if the harm is less than a medical emergency, I say nothing. So, there's always fear. *Fear* of asking for things. *Fear* of telling father anything. *Fear* of ever being myself. Constant *fear*. I'm afraid when I'm angry. Afraid when I'm sad. Afraid even when I'm happy. Afraid every day, all day long. *Immer Angst.*

Heartbreak Hotel

Father plans to build a hotel in our backyard. According to him, it's going to be *my* hotel, so *I'll* be running it. This would be my worst nightmare, because it would mean being stuck with father for much of the rest of my life. His plan horrifies me, because I can't bear the thought of being with him any longer than I have to.

Father would pull out blueprints an architect has drawn up, and force me to look at them with him — *over* and *over*. He'd say something like, "Sit down with me. This is the hotel I'm going to build for you." It's never about what *I* want to do, or what *I* want to learn. It's always what *he* wants. I sit there quietly, hoping he will put away the blueprints as soon as possible — so I can leave.

But he'd be furious that I don't warm up to this hotel project: "How could you not be *grateful?* So many children would be happy and excited!" I sit there quietly and dissociate — just being in my own zone. Not hearing him. Tuning him out. It helps sometimes. But, at other times, it makes things worse.

So, I dread the hotel blueprints. It's another of those occasions when I want to be invisible, to disappear.

The Dark Side

Disturbing Photographs

**Hell, hell is for children,
And you shouldn't have to pay for your love
With your bones and your flesh.** (Benatar/Giraldo/Capps)

Father's volcanic temper and his being so self-centered aren't his only vices. He's also often sexually inappropriate with me, and sometimes outright perverted.

When I'm a child, father presents me to the world as almost a boy. (He probably always wanted a son.) For example, when he drives me to Kurhaus Prasura (p. 43), he has me dress in boys' lederhosen (which have a flap in the front), instead of girls' lederhosen (which have a flap on the side). This alone troubles me. In addition, he takes disturbing snapshots during our trip there. In these photos, I'm holding a soup can in front of me — with the lederhosen flap open. The photos make it appear that I'm *peeing* into the can.

Clearly it isn't *my* idea to pose in this way. I'm on a trip with father to a summer camp/sanatorium. Mother has recently left. I have no idea what's going on, but I'm told to open the flap in front of my lederhosen, and pretend I am peeing into a soup can as if I'm a boy. It's hard to imagine what an adult man is thinking when he tells his 5-year-old daughter to do something like this — and photographs her doing it!

He also takes nude photos of me and my 2-years-younger friend, Margit, a sweet girl whose alcoholic parents, when they visit Bolzitano, stay in the bed-and-breakfast father owns. (Most of father's friends are wealthy professionals from Germany who are alcoholic and, one way or another, are inappropriate in their behavior.) Father sends these pictures, of me pretending to pee in a can and the nudes of Margit and me, to mother(!) She keeps them in a box. After mother dies, my sister Kim finds the box and its contents. Kim is shocked by these creepy pictures, and is so upset that she cries. But, it's not that big a deal to me, because I grew up with father's dark side. (The incident is never discussed with either father or mother, even after I am grown.)

Father and I in front of Kurhaus Prasura Arosa.

Strange Bedfellow

After mother leaves, father makes me sleep beside him. In Europe at the time, a typical double bed has a single frame that contains 2 separate mattresses placed side-by-side. Perhaps father means well initially, because we both miss mother. And, maybe I don't want to sleep alone at first — it's possible — but, this goes on until I'm 13!

A lot happens that shouldn't have happened. There is no actual intercourse, but at times father is definitely inappropriate. Sometimes when he's drunk, he masturbates lying there next to me. Again, I don't know what he could possibly be thinking — but this is plainly sexual abuse.

Back then, father's behavior is confusing to me: Is he merely being free with his own body when he walks around naked in front of me? Or, is he being exploitative in insisting we take nude saunas together? When it comes to nudity, Europe's hippie culture is quite free in the 60's (not that father ever would've been a hippie). Is his behavior just the result of that whole nude culture? Or, does he have a devious and perverted streak? As an adult, I now realize it's partly both. But back then, I was very puzzled by his behavior.

Blackout

If it's time for father to sleep, I have to come to bed too. I'm not allowed to say, "I'm not tired yet", and stay in the kitchen and read. No. If *he's* tired, then *I* have to be tired. Father's bedroom has jet black curtains, because he's so light-sensitive. If he wants the lights off in his bedroom, it means that there can be no light anywhere in the apartment.

Likewise, if he gets up, I must get up. On the other hand, if he doesn't want to get up, I have to stay in bed too. There are many weekend mornings when it's already 10 o'clock, but he's still sleeping (because he got home drunk around 4 AM). It's an ordeal to be wide awake, but still have to lie there next to him. It feels very awkward — and just plain *wrong.*

I might try to sneak off by getting out from under the covers as quietly as I can, and then tiptoeing across the floor. But though it has a small carpet, it's still a little creaky. Many times, father would suddenly wake up and shout at me, "Go lie back down!"

I might answer back, "I'm not tired anymore. I'm going to aunt Martha's house." This would really annoy him, since on weekends he usually has me make breakfast for both of us. Typically, breakfast time on weekends is awful. He's hungover, sullen, and silent. I sit there in fear. Even though a part of me wants to leave, another part feels sad and guilty because he's so unhappy. If he speaks at all over breakfast, he says something depressing like, "There's only you and me in this world; your mother left us. You and me — and no one else." (Not long after, we get Max. Father's weekend lament is then "There's only you, me, and Max in this world.")

He never gets over mother leaving us. His inability to move on emotionally is a big burden for me, because even though I am still a child, it feels like I'm totally responsible for his wellbeing. I think he's too attached to me from the start, even before mother leaves us (see photo on p. 119). Once she's gone, he becomes much *more* emotionally dependent upon me.

Nude in the Sauna

Having learned about saunas from the Russians during the war (when he wasn't fighting them), father builds one in our house. It isn't merely a steam room, but an actual sauna with a big stove that heats up stones, onto which water is thrown. He then uses birch rods to beat himself.

The sauna has showers with special nozzles that provide a strong massage. They are mounted from the sides, as is seen in many modern bathrooms. I have to shower with ice-cold water. He'd say, "This is healthy for you — it's good for your circulation."

Father swears that saunas are the cure for all of life's ills. The sauna *is* great, except that, as mentioned, father makes me sit there in the nude with him. On the one hand, I have no problem with nudity, *per se*. This is now the 1960's. In Europe there is a general culture of nudity. In Germany in particular, whole families go to nude beaches. So, part of me feels that this is normal: *I'm in our sauna with father; he's naked and so am I.* Yet, part of me feels very uncomfortable. Something *isn't* okay. There's a sexualization taking place at the same time as the whole it's-normal-to-be-nude thing. I am very conflicted about sitting there with him.

From ages 7 to 11, I'm often in the sauna with father. He won't allow me to leave until I've been there a long time. When I try to leave, he says things like, "Stay a few more minutes. You're not sweating enough yet." But I'm feeling, *I don't want to stay here anymore. I hate it. Let me out of here!*

In winter, he makes me run barefoot in the snow in my underwear, even naked. He'd say things like, "This is good for you; this is healthy; roll around in the snow — you'll be healthy and won't catch any colds." It may be healthy; but I'm a kid at the time. It's extremely embarrassing to be running barefoot in the snow, wondering whether our neighbors are thinking, *Is she completely nuts?*

Comfort Food

Whatever his conscious or unconscious motives, father's inappropriate behavior causes me a lot of shame and guilt, as well as a negative body image. By the time I am 9 or 10, I already have self-hate when I look in the mirror — I feel disgusted by my appearance. Looking back, I realize now that I was merely a little chubby. But, in those days, I feel enormous. I spend so much time by myself that food becomes very comforting. Food becomes a comfort for father too (along with heavy drinking). So, food is a big deal in both our lives.

Nazi Comrades

As mentioned, father has a number of German friends who stay at his bed-and-breakfast when they are in Bolzitano. During one of her visits, mother tells me they're all Nazis. (She may mean this as a metaphor for any WW II veteran. I don't know for sure. But, that's what she said.)

On a related note, perhaps part of the reason father wants me to speak High German with him is to stay in touch with his "inner SS". I think at some level he wants to be "pure" German, and so he rejects his Austro-Tyrolean identity. (Perhaps part of what attracts him to mother so strongly is that, like his 1st wife, mother is a true Berliner.)

Moral Teachings

And yet, in spite of his failings, father does try to teach me to be a good person. Though he's nominally Catholic, he doesn't attend Mass. He warns me that priests are dangerous, and that I should never trust them. Perhaps he was sexually abused by a priest when he was young. (Maybe that's why he's so inappropriate with me.) Or, perhaps, he knows of others who've been abused. Back then, people don't talk freely about such matters. Whatever the reason, he absolutely can't stand priests. Interestingly, he does trust monks. He tells me that I can trust monks, but not priests.

Although father teaches me I don't need organized religion, he does instill in me a belief in God. For example, whenever we travel to the vacation home in Sulden, we stop at one particular little church. We'd pray silently for a bit. Then he'd light a candle and say, "God is everywhere — you don't have to go to Mass to find Him. You can find Him in Nature, or find Him in a church — quietly when no one else is there."

The Most Loyal Person I Have Ever Known

On the back of a photo of father that one of his girlfriends took, she writes that he's *gütig und verständnisvoll* (kind and understanding). Maybe the hardest part of my childhood is trying to reconcile the duality of good and evil in him.

I vividly remember looking at father and often feeling sorry for him. I see so much pain in his face that I know he too is suffering greatly. In his contemplative moments, which are many, he's not without insight. At some level he realizes the war has permanently damaged him, and that's why he can't help behaving in ways that have driven mother away from us. Hence, my feelings fluctuate from fearing him to pitying him. Part of me believes he wouldn't survive without me — and that I couldn't survive without him, so I have to endure living under his reign of terror. Thus we are both trapped.

Even today, father remains the most influential person in my life. I believe he set the tone for my intimate relationships later on. I've often been attracted to men who are dangerous in one way or another: drug addicts, alcoholics, violent abusers, pathological liars. (Sometimes they have a criminal history.)

But, though father is an extremely difficult man, on the other hand he is always there for me. *Always*. He never abandons me. Though I wind up causing him a great deal of grief, I could still count on him: He shelters me, he feeds me, he stands by my side.

> **Our soul is boundless mercy and when our flawed personality starts to match the breadth, the depth, and power of our soul, we have begun our beginning. Our soul will always be there, waiting for us in ceremony. It will forgive every injury we suffered and caused and hold us in tender embrace. All that was dark will turn to light and we will no longer feel lost.** (*The Masculine Heart,* Robert A Kandarjian)

Father and me in my teen years.

𝔐other

I warmly remember the birthday parties mother has for me when I'm a child. They are always so much fun. There are balloons, cake, games, and other children to play with (mainly my cousins from next door).

Even back then, I realize mother is glamorous. Perhaps as early as age 3, I'm aware that she always looks like a fashion plate — and that this is one of her highest priorities.

Alienation

I've mentioned that mother is an outsider in Bolzitano, and that the other women are always judging her. For example, my hair is a darker shade of blonde for much of the year, but in the summer I have natural highlights. Yet, there are women who accuse mother of *dying* my hair — when I'm only 3 years old!

As another example, they check to see if she goes food shopping in the morning. In Bolzitano, all the matrons shop around 10 or 11 in the morning, so that they can be back home in time to cook a hot meal for their husbands and children, who come home from work or school at lunchtime. Later in the day, the wives prepare dinner, which is usually another hot meal. So, there is a lot of meal preparation involved — at least 2 hours daily. To be candid, I don't think mother is wholeheartedly devoted to their routine of cooking hot meals twice a day.

Also, mother has a lovely svelte figure. Many local women become dowdy once they have children. I think they envy her because of that too.

Mother Wept

My parents were constantly fighting. I remember mother crying a lot, because she's so sensitive. She's crying that night in Munich when she leaves us. And, she's soon in tears whenever she comes back for a visit. Father is annoyed by her tears (no doubt because he's affected by them). He'd grumble something like, "There she goes — crying again."

Survival Suitcase

As noted, during World War II Berlin is the target of heavy bombing — day and night. According to Wikipedia, there are 363 raids from the air over the course of 6 years. Mother goes to bed with a so-called "survival suitcase" next to her. In the middle of the night, when blaring sirens signal that bombing is about to begin, her parents hurriedly take her from bed to a bomb shelter.

Like many of Berlin's children, mother is eventually sent by train to a farm safely away from the bombing raids. It may be while mother is living on a farm that her parents end their marriage. In combination, these childhood events may have been traumatizing for her. If so, father's abuse damages her further.

Care Packages

Besides birthday parties and her fights with father, I don't remember much else about mother during the first 5 years of my life. But, after mother moves to America, we regularly exchange letters. Father monitors my letter-writing to her, and makes sure I include that we *both* miss her — and *both* of us hope she will visit soon.

I recall how happy I was when receiving packages from her 3 or 4 times a year: always for Christmas, Easter, and my birthday, plus maybe once during the summer.

Father at times says something mean like, "Look what kind of mother you have — all she can do is send packages. Why is she sending packages? She doesn't care about us!" Or, "Your mother sends stupid things." But I would think to myself, *She's sending me gifts; that's kind of nice!*

For example, mother might send marshmallows — in part because they represent the excess she *loves* about America. For the very same reason, father despises them (and everything else about America). He thinks they are the worst food you could ever give to a child, so he'd shout, "Marshmallows are garbage!" In his view, most American food is garbage. He yells things like, "Americans will kill themselves with their food!

Watch them eating their f***ing hot dogs and hamburgers and french fries and fast food and McDonald's. You'll see — they're going to kill themselves!"

But then, to father *everything* made in America is garbage. He has been angry at America ever since the war, because the US helped defeat Germany. When mother moves there, he is even angrier. (His fulminating about America is so over the top that I find it amusing.)

He isn't completely wrong about the food, though. The dietary habits of average Americans have been getting worse from the 1950's on. We see the results now with America's high rate of obesity, and rising rates of diabetes and other ailments associated with being overweight. The same thing is happening in many other countries, but America seems to have led the way in this — as in so many other trends, good and bad.

After mother leaves us, she doesn't return for a visit until a few years later, when I'm 8 or 9 (a long time for a child). She doesn't visit again until I'm 11 or 12. From the time I'm 5 until I'm almost 15, I see her on at most 3 occasions, and then for only a couple of days each time.

Fear of Women

When mother does visit, she's still so beautiful and glamorous to me. I'm in sleepy little Bolzitano, whereas she lives in upscale Arlington, Virginia, on the border of dynamic Washington, DC.

As a child, I assume she's successful and happy in America, because when she comes to visit, she has that look of success. Mother's impressive appearance leaves me feeling intimidated by big cities *and* successful women. They seem related, and they both sort of scare me when I'm young. (They continue to scare me well into my adult years.)

For a long time, I generally fear other women. I don't understand them, and I don't know how to relate to them. I begin to learn a little about women when I travel to Amsterdam at age 16. I learn a little more when I'm in my mid-20's while in a program getting off drugs. But, my first in-depth experience of sisterhood (in the broad sense of the term) doesn't occur until I'm in my early 30's (more in Book II).

What *did* I learn from mother? I'm not sure if I learned much from her. It's kind of a big blank. I didn't learn that much from aunt Martha either. Things that a woman usually learns from her mother, I have to learn on my own later in life.

Getting to Know Her

At age 14, I'm arrested in Munich for possession of a couple of grams of hashish (details to come). In consultation with my parents, great aunt Beatrix (who's living in Munich at the time) bails me out of jail and buys a plane ticket for me to be reunited with mother in Arlington. I stay with mother for a little over a year, until she loses patience with my acting out and sends me back to father. It's during this 1st stay in America that I meet her 2nd husband, Knut, a (grandiose) documentary producer who has fathered my newborn sister, Kim.

At first, I think mother and Knut are so cool. When Knut smokes a joint, I get to smoke with him. Mother seems to be okay with that — in the beginning. After awhile, though, she begins having horrible temper tantrums, with lots of yelling and screaming. So, it's in my mid-teens that I see a side of mother that I haven't known before. To my surprise, she behaves in some ways like father, including saying really mean things about me to my face.

Odd Viewpoints

Mother tells me that I "pee like a horse", because I don't simultaneously flush the toilet so as to cover up the sound I'm making. She's kind of weird about this. Years later, my sister Kim and I discuss the topic, because mother says the same thing to her. For some reason, not flushing to mask the sound is poor form.

Mother also has a problem with well-endowed women. She says large breasts are repulsive. While I am attending a German-language school in Washington, DC, I become good friends with Katrin. She's 15, as I am, but Katrin has a rather ample bosom — about 36 double-D. Mother doesn't just dislike big breasts; for some reason, she dislikes the women who have them. It isn't Katrin's fault that she is so well endowed. But, mother can't stand her, because of the size of her bustline. Kim and I talk about this too, but we can't figure out why. (Admittedly, mother eventually discovers Katrin and I naked while partying with 2 boys. This confirms her view of Katrin, but her prejudice was already there.)

Further, mother says men have "this disgusting thing between their legs that flops back and forth". I think she's a little odd about the whole thing. I remember her saying that the best relationship would be marriage to a sailor, because he'd send a check every month, but he'd come home once every 6 months, visit for a few days, and then go back to sea. (This ideal of mother's parallels the relationship of my literary hero, Pippi Longstocking, with her sailor father.)

Mrs. Robinson

One summer, when I'm 9, mother visits the mountain house in Sulden. She arrives wearing a see-through blouse — and no bra. (This is an era when many women are not wearing a bra.) A noticeably younger man accompanies her.

She's then 34; her male companion is in his late 20's (if that). I'm sure he's her lover. It feels strange to me that a younger man is partnered with mother — and yet all of us are in father's house. There are some blurry-boundary issues I'm picking up. Even at that age, I feel the arrangement that weekend somehow isn't right.

Years later, mother says I was acting like a "wild child" during that visit. I was running in and out of the room they were in, keeping an eye on them. I think I wanted to make sure she and her partner were not doing anything inappropriate in my 9-year-old eyes.

Like father, she too is quite free about nudity. She'd change outfits in front of me while I'm living with her in America. This feels kind of strange to me, because I have spent so little time with her before then.

I'm grateful, though, that at times mother is reassuring. For instance, if I tell her I feel fat, she'd encourage me by saying things such as, "You can fix whatever you don't like — there's plenty of time. If you don't like your thighs or your stomach, you can work on slimming them down. And, you can lose weight. So don't worry about it."

Hippie Couture

Mother loves shopping, especially shopping for clothes at up-market stores like Saks Fifth Avenue. So, sometimes we go into Washington, DC to shop together. It's fun for us both because, for example, I like blouses from India, and she does too. Since we have similar taste in clothing, we have no conflict over how I dress. (By contrast, father thinks I'm completely out of my mind for dressing like a hippie.)

But, even though mother is more culturally tolerant than father, she too has a bad temper and, as mentioned, from time to time she would flip-out with no warning. I soon realize that, like father, she isn't a safe person for me to be with.

Blind Spot

When I'm 16, during one of mother's visits to Bolzitano, we're sitting in the kitchen, having a typical mother-daughter conversation. While she's helping me take off one of my boots, a heroin syringe and spoon fall onto the floor(!) Mother goes on talking as if nothing out of the ordinary has happened. At that moment, if I had said, "Oh, mommy, don't you like my boots? Aren't they fabulous!?", she might have responded, "Yes they are, we should go shopping for more boots!"

The syringe is never mentioned, then or later. Not a word. If I discovered a needle on either of my sons, I'd go a little crazy, and say something like, "What are you doing? Are you shooting up drugs? We need to talk about this!" Most importantly, I'd try to get my son help. But, mother never says a word about the syringe, or what it obviously implies I'm doing. Instead, life goes on as before: buying shoes and having fun!

Not a Close Bond

Father dies in May 1980. That December, I pay mother a visit in America. By now, I'm 22 and have a 2½-year-old son, Lukas. She's then living in Easton, Maryland with Rod, her 3rd husband (who is well behaved on this occasion — but I stay for only 2 weeks). Mother is nice to me during this visit, but we still don't have a close bond. It's too hard to establish after all that's happened. Understandably, she has a lot of resentment about the trouble my drug use has caused her by then. Plus, she has always felt like a victim because she has to be married for financial security — not because she really wants to be a wife. Her unhappiness about this puts more strain on our relationship.

Intervention

The next time I see mother is in late 1982, when she comes to South Tyrol. By this time, I have a 2nd son, Johan. My life has been steadily sliding downhill since father's death, increasingly putting her grandsons at risk. In early 1983, via a judge's order, she obtains custody of Lukas and Johan. Utterly broken, I follow her to America to live with her and my sons, while I recover from drug addiction (details to come).

Sabrina

By 1985, I have my sons back, and we're living on our own in Astoria, Queens. Mother asks Sabrina, a family friend from Bolzitano, to live with me and help watch my boys. However, after Sabrina arrives in America, she winds up staying with mother instead. I wonder, *Why is mother keeping Sabrina in Easton, Maryland, rather than letting her live with me in New York as originally planned, when mother knows how hard it is for me to get a reliable babysitter, someone whom I can trust?*

She's been living with mother for about a year when in one of our phone conversations I say to Sabrina, "I'm sorry you don't live with me. I really could use your help, because it's so hard for me to manage without dependable childcare."

Sabrina replies, "I *want* to live with you — I *thought* I was coming to America to watch your children!" She's happy that I've brought this up, because she's been confused herself. She understood from mother that she'd be a nanny to my sons. And yet when she gets here, helping me is never discussed again. Mother has been treating her as if Sabrina is a personal handmaiden, making her do things like wash and blow-dry mother's hair, and be her shopping companion. Sabrina feels she's there just to serve and entertain mother, which is not why she wanted to come to America.

After our talk, Sabrina tells mother that she wants to live with me as previously planned. I suspect another reason she wants to leave mother is that Rod has been behaving inappropriately — as he did with me when I was living under his roof a few years earlier (details below). I'm not sure what's actually happening there, but mother agrees to have Sabrina come live with me. I'm quite happy about this, because now I'll have someone from South Tyrol watching my sons, someone I can relate to personally, and who I feel confident will take good care of them.

Because my kids are in school, Sabrina is able to work part time. A few weeks after she moves in with me, I help her get a sales job at a store in Manhattan where I used to work. She's happy to work retail because, besides the money, she wants to improve her English. She's there mornings, and is home by 3 PM to watch Johan and Lukas. So everything is working out great for all of us.

After not too long, though, mother calls Sabrina and tells her that the Immigration and Naturalization Service (now named U.S. Citizenship and Immigration Services) has sent a letter stating that Sabrina has to leave the country immediately, or she'll be deported back to Italy. Sabrina's scared. She doesn't want to have problems with the INS, which might forever compromise her chance of someday getting a green card.

But, neither Sabrina nor I ever see this letter. We have only what mother tells us over the phone to go by. I suspect that mother is making up the whole thing. She has figured out what to say to deprive me of Sabrina's help. If mother can't have Sabrina as a personal servant, then she's not going to let Sabrina watch Johan and Lukas, her own grandsons.

A few days after mother's phone call, Sabrina decides to go back to Bolzitano. I feel very disappointed and hurt. But, it puts my situation in proper perspective: Although sometimes mother helps me, for which I'm grateful, I can't *rely* on her, because she has a lot of her own emotional issues. For the most part, I have to manage for myself. However, this isn't news — I've grown used to it by now.

Getting A Little Closer

In spite of past hurts, on both sides, by the late 1980's mother and I are regularly getting together on holidays. The boys and I visit her for Thanksgiving. At Christmas, she visits us. She's quite fond of Lukas and Johan, and treats them very well.

But, though mother and I are getting a little bit closer, we still aren't that close. One Thanksgiving (maybe it's in 1988), she invites the 3 of us to spend the holiday with her. We take a bus to Maryland, where mother is then living. She picks us up at the bus station, and drops us off at the house of a friend of hers — someone we hardly know. Then mother disappears!

So, *this* is Thanksgiving. As nightfall approaches, her friend says to me, "Don't worry — you can sleep here." I'm thinking, *Okay, but why are we here at all?*

It all feels so strange. I have no idea where mother has gone. She may have had a date with a man she does not want us to know about. Or, maybe she does not want him to know about us. I can't be sure — she just does odd things like this.

Night Flight

In the early 1990's, I'm finally back in school, and I'm in therapy as well. I think mother has started to respect me a little more, because I'm working on improving myself, and on making things better for the boys. So, mother and I continue to grow closer. She's visiting us more often than just at Christmastime, and we're all getting along well.

As part of their divorce settlement (because of his infidelity), Rod has bought her an apartment in Rockville, Maryland, which is just north of Washington, DC. To meet ongoing expenses, she gets a job at an airline as part of their Dulles Airport staff. Sometime in 1992, mother becomes a flight attendant. (Kim and I aren't happy about this, because too much could happen.)

But mother really enjoys traveling, especially flying. Now anytime she has a problem, she can get on a plane and fly away. Further, she loves the leather shoes, pleated skirts, and crisp white blouses that comprise her uniform. In other words, mother really likes being a flight attendant.

Meanwhile, Kim comes to New York City to study journalism. At first she lives in the school dormitory, but this is an added financial burden. So around the time that mother becomes a flight attendant, Kim moves in with us in Queens, and stays until she's finished with school. She helps care for Lukas and Johan, and I don't charge her rent.

Mother, Kim, the boys, and I celebrate Christmas 1993 together in Astoria. Two weeks later, mother is working on a flight from Washington, DC to an airport in the Midwest. It's a freezing cold night, the atmosphere is icy, and there's some fog along the route. A lot of airports in the region have closed because of the bad weather. But the flight mother is on, with a crew of 3 (including her) and a mere 5 passengers, departs anyway.

The subsequent government report indicates that the captain is inexperienced in general, and in particular isn't experienced with the plane he's piloting (a new model), flying in bad weather at night, or emergency landings. During the past year, he flunked his 1st try at a flight-simulator test of emergency landing procedures. The examiner notes that he became "unusually nervous", and made errors in procedure — even in the *simulated* test.

During the plane's approach to the airport, the 1st officer fails to provide certain information in a timely manner. This causes the captain to lose his cool (as revealed by the cockpit voice recording). The captain then makes several procedural errors, and as a result the plane stalls. He errs further in his attempts to recover from the stall.

A little more than a mile from the runway, the now rapidly descending plane hits the treetops of a wooded area, cartwheels about 175 feet into a large commercial building, and then bursts into flames, engulfing the building as well. It takes firefighters almost an hour to finally extinguish the conflagration.

Mother, the captain, and the 1st officer all die on impact. Two of the 5 passengers succumb to smoke inhalation. Miraculously, the other 3 passengers — a husband, wife, and their young child — have only minor injuries and exit the plane just before it goes up in flames.

Mother would have been 59 in March of that year. She sometimes said that she didn't want to ever get old. I think coping with old age would've been a real struggle for her, especially if she were to become infirm. She wanted to remain young and beautiful. To always look good, with a body that's still in shape.

In the end, she gets her wish.

Mother with me on her right and my cousin Astrid on her left.

𝕰𝖆𝖗𝖑𝖞 𝕬𝖉𝖔𝖑𝖊𝖘𝖈𝖊𝖓𝖈𝖊
Body Image

From the age of 11 on, I eat too much comfort food, especially pudding. By age 12, I weigh over 130 pounds. This isn't a great deal of weight, but back then most children are skinny by today's standards. Although not the biggest girl in my class at school, I'm probably heavier than all but 2. Being athletic, I'm not flabby. But I'm thick, and quite uncomfortable in my body. I become increasingly depressed, and no longer function well in school.

A Room of My Own

At age 13, I finally get my own bedroom — only because Petra, father's latest girlfriend, starts sleeping in his bed. Petra is probably in her early 30's at the time (about the same age as mother). Previously, she was married to a wealthy Italian businessman who lived in Trieste, which is now on the northeastern border of Italy. But for centuries prior to World War I, Trieste was part of Austria, and Petra herself is ethnically Austrian. Her husband was quite wealthy, and she learned to cook the Friulian cuisine of Trieste to please him. Father too likes her Friulian cooking. As an added attraction, from father's point of view, when Petra is drunk (which is not infrequently), she might hop on a table and do a striptease.

Café Odeon

Café Odeon is a bistro near the center of Bolzitano, where local kids go to have fun. From the age of 14, I spend a lot of time there. It's where I meet Fabio (another lost soul).

On any given day, a bunch of us would sit around one of Café Odeon's large tables. There are probably 30 or 40 of us in the whole group. On a weekday, usually only 3 to 6 of us are present at the same time. But on weekends, perhaps as many as 20 of us would surround one of the tables.

Although I'm 14, I can legally drink beer at Café Odeon. As mentioned, in Europe at the time there's no minimum age for buying beer or wine. A 12-year-old could ask for beer and be served. We'd order huge pitchers of beer for the table. Who-ever has money would pay.

We're all so young and carefree as the hours go by. Someone might have marijuana or hashish. We'd leave Café Odeon and stroll along one of the nature walks on the outskirts of town, getting high smoking large joints of marijuana, or hash pipes with a huge bowl, soaking in nature, and then walking back into town — laughing and having a blast. Fabio, who is then 17, is always in the group.

Me And My Shadow

Now that I'm 14, I've become more curious about boys. There are parties I'd go to, sometimes hitchhiking with friends to different towns to attend them. But, I'm terrified of running into father — I'm always afraid that he's following me. One time when I'm hitchhiking with a friend, father pulls over in the wine-colored Peugeot he owns at the time. I almost die of embarrassment and fear. I'm wondering, *Oh, my God, what do I do now?*

Of course, we have to get into his car. (Living with father feels like I've been sentenced to life imprisonment.) But this one time, he doesn't say a word, other than to ask us where we want to go. He drives us there in silence. This is quite un-usual. For some reason, on that day there is no volcanic eruption, no beating, no screaming. Maybe he is resigned to my growing up — on that occasion anyway. (His intervals of reasonableness never last long.)

Sexual Sleepwalking

My first experience of actual sexual intercourse is being rap-ed at age 14. One night I simply don't want to go home — but I don't have any other place to go. Marcus, my boyfriend of the time, suggests I stay at his friend Andy's house.

However, Marcus cautions, "Andy is a womanizer. You have to firmly tell him to leave you alone."

I reply, "Sure — no problem."

Andy is 19 and handsome. He has 2 single beds in his bedroom, and we go to sleep in separate beds. But in the mid-dle of the night, Andy climbs into my bed and starts putting moves on me. I say to him, "Andy, leave me alone. You're Marcus's friend; I'm Marcus's girlfriend. This isn't right."

Yet, Andy keeps forcing himself on me. I remember crying and begging him, "Please don't do this." But, he won't stop.

So, this is my first time. If I'd reported him to the police, Andy might have gotten a long prison sentence because, regardless of any other factors, I'm only 14 when this happens. Instead, I just leave the next morning as if nothing has happened.

However, more broadly speaking, Andy isn't the 1st man to sexually violate me. He's just the 1st to penetrate me. Father has already violated me so many times — in the ways he's touched me, in the places he's held me, in the things he's made me do. So, when Andy rapes me, I don't feel that any-one would respect my saying *no*. I don't feel I even have the right to say *no*.

Porous Boundaries

As is too often the case for young people who've been abu-sed, I grow up without a solid boundary between where the rights of others end, and my rights begin. Because of this, a number of adult men are able to take advantage of me when I'm in my early teens.

For example Elmar and Ralf, who are in their 30's, run Tra-jet, a Sulden nightclub. Tourists would go there after skiing in the Alps all day. But locals go there too, because it's a happening place. At 14, I start going to Trajet to get in on the fun. Father knows about it, but he likes Elmar and Ralf, so he allows me to go.

One night at Trajet, I've been drinking so much that I barely know what's going on. I realize I should go home, but I'm in no condition to get there on my own. I wake up the next mor-ning lying naked in Ralf's bed. Elmar is there too. I know I've had sex, but I'm not even sure if it was with one or both of them. While I'm looking for my clothes, which are strewn about the floor, Ralf comments, "Look at her small breasts — they stand up straight!" Both men laugh. I'm mortified.

Feeling gross and hungover, I walk home by myself wonder-ing, *How do I explain to father where I've spent the night?*

But, to my surprise, once I tell him that I was with Elmar and Ralf, he doesn't go crazy. I guess they're okay in his book because they aren't hippies or Communists. (However, he's *never* predictable.)

There are other adult men who take advantage of my vulnerability back then. I don't make a big deal over it, but I feel a great amount of shame for a long time afterward. Because of all the abuse, my attitude about men becomes: *We can have sex, but don't fall in love with me, because I'm not going to stick around. I don't want the wedding and white dress. I certainly don't want to be walked down the aisle by father. I'm not that kind of girl. I don't have those dreams. That's exactly what I don't want. Just the thought of it makes me nauseous.*

As a result of such experiences, sex in my early teen years becomes a casual matter for me. My partners are nice boys — they don't treat me badly. But I have no real feelings for them. I'm not in love with them, and I'm not interested in having a committed relationship.

Runaway

Early in 1973 (before I get arrested in Munich and sent to America), I run away from home for the 1st time. I desperately want out of that house. Father has been promising me for years that I would have my own bedroom. He's built an extension to our home, and we now have 5 bedrooms, 2 living rooms, a huge kitchen, 2 bathrooms, and a spacious balcony. There has been *plenty* of room for some time. So, why was I still sleeping in his bed until age 13? As mentioned, it's not until his girlfriend Petra starts sleeping next to him that I'm finally able to have my own bedroom.

But, his behavior is still driving me away. For example, now that I do have my own bedroom, I hang on the wall a calendar with pictures of musicians I'm a fan of (including some black musicians). Father has a fit and rips the calendar down off the wall, calling all of these musicians "hippies" and "Communists". He is so worked up that he practically destroys my room, including smashing bottles of red nail polish, making it look like there's blood all over the walls and floor.

Further, there's the whole history of his physical and verbal abuse. By age 14, I simply don't want to live under the same roof with him — with or without my own room. One night in the spring of 1973, I pack my clothing into a couple of airline carry-on bags. I plan to just sneak out the door. But, father walks into my bedroom and discovers me packing. He starts shouting furiously. Then he opens the balcony door, and flings the contents of my carry-on bags off the balcony. (My clothing gets stuck on branches of the trees below.)

I'm shouting too — because I'm terrified of him. I cry out, "Papi, please, I promise I am going to be good. I won't ever do this again. I don't really want to leave you!"

Now in tears, I beg and plead — trying everything I can to placate him. But, he continues to act like a maniac, pacing back and forth on the balcony while yelling at me. My fear is that in his rage he will pick me up and throw *me* off the balcony too.

Uncle Hubert hears this uproar, and comes rushing over to try to rescue me. In a reversal of roles, uncle Hubert now is the one who is doing the shouting: "What is *wrong* with you, Werner? Calm down — stop this carrying on!"

After a time, father finally goes back inside. Uncle Hubert and I then go downstairs. I climb the tree (something I've had lots of experience doing) and, with help from uncle Hubert, I get my carry-on bags and clothing down.

In spite of father's tantrum, or perhaps because of it, that night I set out from home on foot. Nine years after mother leaves him, I leave him too. I'm feeling at peace — even though I'm not sure where I'll spend the night(!) I think to myself, *My God, I've done this. I've actually gotten away from this maniac.* I feel for the 1st time in my life that I can be myself and do whatever I want.

𝕱𝖆𝖇𝖎𝖔

A Certain Mystique

Fabio and I meet at Café Odeon, as mentioned, when he's 17 and I'm 14. Though he's ethnically Austrian, Fabio reminds me of Bob Marley, because he has beautiful black hair that falls almost to his navel (the kind of wavy hair that every woman wants for herself). He's slim, about 6' tall, has brown eyes and full lips, and wears washed-out jeans and cowboy boots. He usually sports a loose-hanging long-sleeved tee-shirt, like Mick Jagger. As a fashion accent, Fabio wears a silver bracelet and silver ring.

In a word, Fabio is *gorgeous*.

After his alcoholic father, Armin, kicks him out of the house, when he's 15, Fabio quits school. I don't think he ever gets past the 8th grade. But, he doesn't need more school to get by in life. He's such a pretty boy that women often pay his way.

For example, while still in his mid-teens, he lives for a time in Switzerland with a woman in her 20's. She takes good care of him. I think she lets him drive her fancy Mercedes. I know she gives him fine clothing and other expensive gifts. After he returns from Switzerland, he starts dating Antonia, a nurse at the local hospital. Antonia is about 19, and by then he's 17. She too takes care of him.

When I begin dating, I definitely don't want another man in my life who screams, acts scary, and is at times violent. (Yet, after father's gone, I sometimes choose such men.)

In complete contrast, Fabio is a quiet man. I never hear him yell or even raise his voice. He's always relaxed, and he makes people close to him feel safe, instead of afraid (the opposite of father). I remember thinking, *He's quiet and mysterious, but he exudes a sense of calm. I like that — I really want to get to know him.*

Fabio would sit quietly in Café Odeon for lengthy spells, just smoking cigarettes. We'd hang out and smoke and drink together. Afterward, he'd walk me home. We'd say very little, just silently strolling together.

Hippie Pad

That chilly night in spring, when father throws my things off the balcony, turns out to be a turning point in my life. I'm 14 years old, I have nowhere to go, and I'm wondering to myself, *What do I do now?* I decide to go to Fabio's place, because he feels so safe to be with. Although his father has kicked him out of the main house, Fabio's mother, Gerda, allows him to live in a small house in the rear of their property. I walk the 2 miles to where Fabio lives, and find that he's not there. But I don't care. I'd have sat there for eternity to wait for Fabio. It's that important for me to be with him that night.

Fabio gets home at 2 or 3 in the morning. He says something like, "What are you doing here, baby?", and then leads me inside his place. I can still visualize how it's arranged: There are only 2 rooms, a main room and a kitchen. The main room has 3 mattresses on the floor, laid out like an I-shaped sofa. (There are always drugs, burning incense, and space for people to crash.) Soon the Rolling Stones are singing *Sister Morphine* on Fabio's stereo. I know I'm "home".

The kitchen has a wood-burning stove, but there's no toilet or other plumbing. Water is brought in by bucket from an outdoor faucet. There isn't even an outhouse. The backyard is the "bathroom". The whole setup is pretty primitive — but I think it's great!

What's important to me is that I've escaped from father. I don't care that I have no shower, no running water, and no toilet. If I have to pee in the backyard for the rest of my life, I'm okay with that, because Fabio's pad is the one place where I feel completely safe.

Besides his being quiet and calm, something else that draws me closer to Fabio is his not trying to get me into bed right away (unlike the others). That 1st night I spend at Fabio's house, though we sleep on the same mattress, he doesn't attempt to touch me. He's completely respectful. He just wants me to be safe. After we get up in the morning, he makes me breakfast with coffee.

It's a different kind of relationship. I feel taken care of by Fabio, so I live with him there for awhile.

Coming Home

I have $100 when I leave father. After a time, I move out of Fabio's place and rent a $50 per month room. Claudia (my friend Lenora's mother) comes to my room and tells me father is very unhappy and wants me to return home. I reply that I don't think this is a good idea, because he's not going to change. It's going to be the same thing. He'll yell, scream, and generally act crazy I don't want to live like that anymore. But, Claudia convinces me to go back to father.

I return and tell father I'm going to try to live with him one last time. This is the wrong thing to say. Father immediately explodes and starts shouting at me. Now that I'm back, I never know if he's going to beat me again. From age 14 on, it only gets worse. I ask myself, *Why did I return? It's never going to get better!* Living with him feels as if doomsday could come at any moment.

Father Meets and Greets Fabio

By now, I'm madly in love with Fabio. I'm always by his side at Café Odeon. I don't think father would have approved of anyone, because he's so possessive of me. But, Fabio is the *worst* choice possible, from father's point of view, because Fabio is a drug-using hippie.

One day, while I'm sitting at one of the big tables at Café Odeon, someone tells me that father is standing by the bar. This can't be good news, and I'm very embarrassed. (It's another moment when I want to be invisible.) Suddenly, he strides over to our table and, without warning, punches Fabio in the nose — literally breaking it. I think, *Oh my God — he has gone crazy again!* There's blood everywhere, and I'm feeling terrible for Fabio.

No Exit

Father tries his best to separate us, but his efforts just push me closer to Fabio. He sometimes stalks us — I never know when he will suddenly show up. Fabio and I could be in a nightclub together, and I might turn around and see father standing at the bar.

I want to crawl under a table whenever father creates an outrageous public scene. He accuses everyone else of being a "bad influence" — Fabio, cousin Astrid, the Beatles, *etc*, but only rarely reflects (and then drinks to forget) that his own behavior is causing me to rebel.

As an adolescent, I can't wait to turn 18, because I feel that then father will no longer follow me around, chase me out of nightclubs, beat up my boyfriend, and generally embarrass me in public — things he's done so many times.

Heroin: The 'Miracle Drug'

I'm 15 when I use heroin for the 1ˢᵗ time — with the help of Fabio and his friend Heidi. I beg them for it. I want nothing more than to be part of what they seem to belong to: the happy and mellow club.

The 2 of them debate whether they should hit me up or not. They finally agree to do it. To extract the heroin, they grind up in a spoon "Peshawar pills" (morphine tablets from Pakistan). They then add water and heat the mixture with a flame until the pills dissolve. I think it's Fabio who shoots me up, but I'm no longer sure. What I am sure of is that although I quickly vomit, I then have feelings I have never had before: I feel okay *being me!* Okay being in my own skin. No fear; no shame. A sense of freedom and safety that I'm feeling for the 1ˢᵗ time in my life.

These little white pills are magic. When I'm high on heroin, there's no more pain. And, it doesn't block just physical pain; it blocks emotional pain too. Right then and there, I feel that my survival depends on continuing to use it. Heroin makes me numb to the trauma I've suffered from being abandoned by mother at age 5, and being physically, emotionally, and sexually abused by father for the 10 years since then. I'm able to have dinner with father without fear or even discomfort. The issues we've had in the past don't matter to me anymore. No more *immer Angst*.

From the time I'm 12 until I start using heroin at 15, I don't speak much, not even with friends. I'm the quiet one, the shy one, the one who's always afraid of saying the wrong thing, of doing something awkward or inappropriate. I'm constantly judging and censoring myself, feeling I'm too clumsy, too fat, too unimportant, that I don't fit in, and that people don't want me around.

Heroin puts an end to all my self-doubts. When I'm high on heroin, I feel I fit in, like I'm a normal human being. I lose my social insecurity. For the first time, I'm able to talk freely in front of other people. I feel energetic and empowered. All told, I feel *good* for a change!

Soon, I'm hooked on heroin.

An Identity of My Own

Last, but not least, after a lifetime of not having an identity other than "Werner's daughter", I finally have an identity of my own: I'm a junkie. (Pretty much everyone Fabio and I hang out with is moving in this direction.)

I overdose twice. On one occasion, I'm with Fabio and Heidi at his place. I'm looking at myself in a wall mirror as I slowly sink to the floor. I remember expecting to die then and there — and feeling completely at peace about it (at age 15). Although Fabio and Heidi do nothing to revive me, after awhile I regain consciousness. At that point, I feel very disappointed to still be alive.

Heroin and Intimacy

I love Fabio unconditionally. But, because both of us are heavy users of heroin, we're not emotionally present for each other. We're using drugs to avoid dealing with the childhood trauma we each have had. Unlike the situation with some of my lovers later in life, I'm never repelled by physical intimacy with Fabio. However, because we're doing drugs so much back then, I honestly don't remember what was going on in the bedroom during the 7 years we lived together (not withstanding that we had 2 sons). It's as if we're both in a fog. I do know that I don't fly into a rage when he touches me (as will often happen in future relationships).

Older, but Wiser

Now that I'm a parent myself, I can better understand father's dim view of Fabio. At the beginning of our romance, I'm just a kid of 14. Fabio, who soon turns 18, isn't going to school, but he doesn't have a job either — and he has no plans to get one.

Father knows, as does everyone else in Bolzitano, that Fabio is using hard drugs. But, he's far from the only young person in town who's a user. Back then (the 1970's) the so-called *French Connection*, which smuggles heroin into Europe via Marseilles, is operating at its peak. Local people are also traveling to, and returning with drugs from, places like Amsterdam, Afghanistan, and Iran. So, there are plenty of sources of drugs in Bolzitano.

But, everyone blames Fabio, especially parents. A lot of them, not only father, feel that he's a bad influence on their children. They view him as the Devil, the worst of the worst. (I now regret that my relationship with Fabio must have been particularly painful for father.)

Although Fabio is not nearly as bad as others make him out to be, it's true that he's a hippie who lacks ambition. In retrospect, I think he was a chronically depressed young man. He grew up in a home with an alcoholic father who beat both Fabio and his mother.

His mother, Grerda, is codependent. She sacrifices herself for Armin and Fabio by having 2 jobs, sometimes 3. She works as a server in a local restaurant. Plus, they have a farm with livestock, which she feeds herself. And, she also does all the housework. In other words, she does everything.

In Armin's younger days, he was an avid hunter. He still has guns, rifles, and other hunting gear. But, due to his alcohol abuse, his hunting license has been taken from him by the authorities. Afterward, he becomes increasingly depressed. I remember seeing Armin shuffling about town, not saying anything, and looking almost like a zombie — even when he was still in his early 40's.

Armin doesn't accomplish much in life. Even when sober, he isn't a good role model for Fabio. And, Gerda is a big enabler. She brings Fabio breakfast every day. (While I'm living with him, she brings *both* of us breakfast every day.) Perhaps she feels guilt and pity because he's been kicked out of the house by Armin, but I know she doesn't push Fabio to get a job. Fabio never actually does much of anything. Eventually, he starts dealing drugs as his livelihood. Now that I'm a parent myself, I can appreciate why a father would not want his daughter to be with Fabio.

But still, he's charming, handsome, and charismatic. *I want to be his partner for life.*

Coming to America 1
Munich Holiday

One summer day in 1973 (before I move in with Fabio), I tell father I want to go on vacation to Munich. Although in his view a summer vacation should be spent in the mountains, he's in a good mood that day. So, he gives me 300 German marks, which is worth a few hundred US dollars in today's money. (This includes train fare, because he doesn't want me to hitchhike.)

Father is so strict at times, and yet at other times he's quite permissive. What father gives his 14-year-old daughter a wad of cash to go on a frolic in a foreign city?

Maybe he figures that at least I won't be with Fabio. In fact, I do make this trip with 2 male friends other than Fabio. Although I haven't used heroin yet, I'm already smoking pot and hashish. When the 3 of us get to Munich, we buy mescaline and hash. I wind up falling asleep in The English Garden, which is like Central Park in New York City. When I wake up, I don't have 300 marks anymore — instead, I have 100. The 2 guys I've been traveling with, who I thought are my friends, have stolen the rest of my money.

I'm 14 and all alone. While wandering about Munich, I encounter another 2 friends from South Tyrol. They're going to hitchhike to Amsterdam. I decide to join them, but I forget that I have hash in my pocket. On the German Autobahn, we get picked up by police. After searching me and finding 3 grams of hash, they arrest and jail me.

I'm terrified of being sent home to father. So I tell the police that I live in the United States with mother (whom I haven't seen in years, and even then for only a couple of days).

Because of the delay my evasion causes, I spend an interesting 2 nights in jail. The 1st night I'm there by myself until a streetwalker comes in. She's followed by a young woman accused of forging narcotics scrips. Then another streetwalker comes in. She keeps saying her "honey" will get her out. It seems that the only incarcerated women are those who've offended public morals regarding sex and drugs.

After the police contact mother, she calls her mother's twin sister, my great aunt Beatrix, who's still living in Munich at the time. As noted earlier, I'm released from jail into Beatrix's custody. After mother consults with father, they decide to have Beatrix put me on a plane to Arlington, where I will be living with mother after all.

Anomie in Arlington

Father feels this is all a conspiracy to separate us, and yet he goes along with sending me to America. It will get me away from the Café Odeon crowd — especially Fabio. And, maybe mother is willing because she feels guilty that her absence from my life might be part of the reason I've gone astray.

As mentioned, mother is now married to Knut. When I arrive, he's 33, she's 38, and Kim is only 1 or 2 months old. Knut is something of an intellectual, and he talks a lot about his accomplishments (which are sort of impressive — but not *that* impressive) as a producer of documentaries.

I'm finally reunited with mother. And, I have a baby sister. Plus, I'm smoking pot with my new stepfather(!) At first, mother seems okay with this — we're one big happy family.

But, mother doesn't really know what to do with me. A month later, she has me return to father. And yet, in October father says to me, "You may as well go back to your mother", and he sends me back to her. (It seems that neither of them want me, now that I'm a drug-using teenager.)

Still unsure what to do with me, mother decides that we're going to Australia to stay with grandmother Frieda, though Kim is only a few months old. (As noted, often mother would travel when things get difficult or awkward for her.)

We arrive in Australia in October 1973. As discussed earlier, on New Year's Eve I'm dancing with Frieda while listening to her sing *My Way,* and at the end of the evening I carry her up the stairs to her bedroom.

Aside from a few occasions like New Year's Eve, I'm depressed most of the year I live with mother. I miss father, Fabio, my cousins, and my friends. And I miss Bolzitano — the feel of grass under my bare feet as I walk around the backyard, or up a mountain, or the smell of the Alpine air. (As this is written, I still miss them all.)

Age 15, Arlington, Virginia.

While we're in Australia, grandfather Hubert passes on, in his mid-90's. I miss him too, and am very sad that I can't be at his funeral.

The whole time we're there, no one ever asks, "Why isn't Marlena in school? Why isn't she doing anything with her life?" It's all okay. I don't have to study, or to go to school — after all, I'm traveling the world with mother.

School Daze

In February 1974, mother and I return to America. The issue finally arises: *Marlena needs to go to school!* At first, I attend Washington, DC's *Deutsche Schule* (German School), a ritzy private academy, most of whose students are sons and daughters of German diplomats. Because I'm 15, I'm enrolled in the 10th grade. But I'm still at the 8th grade level in math, while the other students are at the high school level in physics, math, and Latin. I'm completely lost.

After I've floundered for 2 months, mother has me transferred to a public high school in Arlington. Public school in America is a completely new experience for me. I like it because there is so much diversity, and there are girls in the restroom smoking hash. Plus, there's a swimming pool, so I get to take swimming classes. I think, *Wow, this is great. I feel at home!*

I've never seen behavior like this. In math class some of the students are tripping on LSD(!) I feel, *Yay — everything I've been doing that was deemed so horrible and that made me so marginalized in Bolzitano seems to be the norm in the US!*

My life with father was unstructured by comparison with how other people lived in Bolzitano. But, now that I'm in America, a lack of structure is commonplace. The home of every kid I visit is incredibly disorganized. No one bothers to make their bed, there are scattered clothes everywhere, and no one seems to have regular meal times. I think to myself, *I guess people can live and be happy without having to follow all of South Tyrol's norms.*

Disillusionment

Now that I'm living with mother day-in and day-out, my image of her is diminished. Since I was 5, I have had this fantasy that my beautiful, sophisticated mother is living a glamorous life in a faraway big city — an ideal woman living an ideal life. Now that I'm finally reunited with her, I discover that she doesn't have all that much going for her. She isn't happy, and she doesn't feel good about herself. Further, I learn that she's as temperamental as father — and as unpredictable. One day she loves me and is very nice. The next day she has a huge fit and calls me horrible names.

In a normal parent-child relationship, a child's realization that a parent has faults (as all of us do) comes gradually. But since mother and I were apart for so long, learning of her shortcomings so suddenly comes as a shock.

I've always known I'd have to depend on myself — not a man. I've been practically self-sufficient since I was 5, when I promised myself I'd never get married. Seeing mother struggling with her 2nd marriage that isn't going well, reinforces my determination to never marry.

Birthday Surprises

For my 16th birthday, father sends me a gold chain and pendant. It's obviously very expensive. I start to cry. He can't control his temper, but he tries to compensate by being so generous. Seeing my tears, mother shares that she has similar conflicted feelings about his love for us — and our love for him. I think to myself, *Yes, but you were able to leave — you weren't forced to spend your childhood with his craziness.*

Shortly after my birthday, mother also surprises me. She tells me she's bought me a plane ticket back to Italy — and it leaves the next day! Then she locks me in my bedroom in order to keep me confined until morning. At that moment, I feel, *Oh, I'm such an inconvenience to your wonderful Washington life, with your 50 pairs of beautiful high heels, your lovely white blouses, and your tailored pencil skirts!*

In fairness to mother, I must admit that my moving from Bolzitano to Arlington doesn't end my rebelliousness. I often go to DC to get drugs (though not heroin) from one of my several boyfriends. And, there's the nude party with Katrin and 2 boys. I've been pretty out-of-control.

I beg mother's permission to say goodbye to a friend in the building that I've been commuting to school with. She allows me to do this, and I repay her trust by instead taking a bus into DC. Soon, mother has the police looking for me, since DC isn't a safe place for a girl who's just turned 16, and hangs out with drug dealers in rundown areas of town.

I stay with Charles for a few nights. But, he has girlfriends besides me. I decide that I'm better off, after all, going back to father. When I return to mother's house, the police are there.

Mother won't speak to me — except to call me a "whore". She doesn't even come to the airport. Instead, she has Knut drop me off.

During a layover in London, I debate with myself whether to simply disappear in the UK. (I've learned to speak English pretty well during my stay in America.) But, I don't have the courage to flee. What would I do in London? I'm 16, and I have no money. Resigned, I board the connecting flight to Munich.

When father picks me up at the airport (with Petra, naturally), the first thing he says to me is, "Thanks for ruining my life again!" Obviously, things haven't gotten any better. I silently say to myself, *Don't worry about it, father — I'm not going to stick around for long.*

𝔐agical 𝔐ystery 𝔗our

The next time I run away from father, I get much farther than the backyard of Fabio's parents; farther even than The English Garden in Munich. (From age 14 on, I have a pattern of leaving father and then coming back; mother does also — even after she remarries.)

Things at home are still really bad. Petra hates me and, frankly, I don't care for her. From the start, she's been jealous of father's strong emotional attachment to me, which is still obvious in spite of all the trouble I've caused him.

Astrid, who's really my only witness to all the pain father is inflicting on me, comes up with an escape plan — I'm to be kidnapped! She knows a farmer in the mountains near Bolzitano. He'll let me live in his barn for 2 years, until I turn 18 and am legally free of father's control. That she'd devise so extreme a plan is a measure of how painful living with father has been for me. But, not wanting to hide in some farmer's barn for 2 years, I decide against it.

A month or 2 after I'm back living with father, a less drastic plan begins to take shape: I'll run away to Amsterdam with some local kids who are planning a trip there. Gio, a boy I like a lot, owns one of those 'hippie vans' that are popular in the 1970's. Europeans are driving these vans everywhere — to places as far away as Kabul, Afghanistan and Kathmandu, Nepal. The driver, and passengers if any, can sleep in the back, so these vans are kind of like an early RV.

There are 2 other guys going on the trip, and 2 girls besides myself: Iris, age 17; and Fabio's friend Heidi, now age 20. So 6 of us in total are making the trip to Amsterdam.

Once we're underway, I write a letter to Astrid. I'm sure father will intercept my note if I send it in care of aunt Martha and uncle Hubert. In the letter, I say goodbye to Astrid, and tell her that I'm on my way to Greece. I don't want father to accuse her of helping me to leave, and I don't want him to know that I am actually in Amsterdam. Trying to cover all the bases, I also write to father telling him too that I'm traveling to Greece.

Gio's plan is to continue on to Hammerfest, Norway, one of the northernmost cities in Europe. He wants me to accompany him, and I want to go too. But Heidi, as the oldest in our group, is the mother hen who wants to control everyone and everything. She's very strident, and I'm intimidated by her. She tells me, "You're not going to Norway; you're staying in Amsterdam with me." I don't have the courage to say *no* to her — she just takes over.

Dutch Treats

When we get to Amsterdam, Gio's deeply disappointed that I'm not going with him to Hammerfest, and I'm sad that he'll be all alone. But Heidi's made plans for me to stay with her and a friend of hers in Amsterdam. She says to me, "You're only 16. You'll come with me, and I'll make sure you're okay." But, when I ask Heidi if Iris, who's just 17, can come with us, Heidi says *no*. (Later, Iris dies of a drug overdose.)

Regardless, the whole trip is interesting for me, since I've never traveled for an extended period on my own. When the van breaks down in Zürich, Switzerland, we stay the night waiting for it to be fixed. Walking about early the next morning, we come upon fresh milk and bread outside a restaurant that is not yet open. Not having much money, we steal some milk and bread from the restaurant's doorway. Heidi's the leader of the pack, of course. She doesn't steal just milk and bread; she also steals a newspaper, and comments, "Now *this* is a perfect breakfast. We even have a paper to read!"

Once we're in Amsterdam, Heidi starts dominating me in earnest. She can be fun to be with, but I have to dance to her tune the whole time I'm there. She decides when we go out, where we go, what we do, when we sleep, *etc.* She calls all the shots (like father).

Houseboat

Heidi's friend in Amsterdam seems a bit creepy to me, but he has a large houseboat. Several other hippies live on it. Heidi sleeps in his bedroom, which is the largest. I suppose they have sex. (I don't pay much attention to such matters at the time.) They give me a tiny room, but at least I don't have to have sex with anyone. Heidi does look out for me in that way.

The others on the boat are drug addicts too. I've taken all of my jewelry with me from home — some expensive gold chains and other fine jewelry father has given me — because I think I'm never going back. Soon, all of my valuables are stolen by one or more of the others.

Now that I have no money, or anything else of value, I have to work for Heidi to earn my room and board. Heidi is a savvy businesswoman, and somehow she has enough money to buy a big brick of hashish. I remember her dividing up the hash into small chunks and packaging them. She also has LSD in a form called "windowpane", because it comes in clear little squares that are taped onto sheets of paper. (Looking back, I wonder if she got the seed money by selling my jewelry.) I have to deal hash and LSD for Heidi, spending every night outside either Galaxy or Tulipmania, 2 of Amsterdam's more popular nightclubs. While I'm selling the LSD — with all the proceeds turned over to her — Heidi is inside sitting on fancy cushions, smoking opium and snorting heroin.

My Madame

Heidi has me stay outside selling drugs until 2 or 3 every morning — at age 16. Although no sex is involved, in a sense Heidi is like my virtual madame. She'd come outside and ask, "How much did you sell?" If, for example, I have only 20 Dutch guilder (about $20), she'd get angry and yell at me. And, she doesn't allow me to rest. I can't go inside the club and sit down and relax — I have to stay outside and sell.

One day I lose about 20 windowpanes of LSD. The strip of paper they are on falls on the ground somewhere. A guy who's also selling drugs finds the windowpanes, and exclaims, "Wow — I found some acid!"

Hearing this, I say to him, "Oh, they're mine! You need to give them back to me, because I'm in trouble for losing them." But it's a cutthroat scene, so he doesn't return them. Instead, he replies, "That's too bad: If you lost them, you lost them. I'm selling them now." When Heidi finds out, she's furious with me.

A good deal of the time, I'm exhausted and undernourished. The houseboat is always damp, and my 'bed' is a tiny mattress. When it rains overnight, I wake up in the morning with water dripping onto me from the ceiling. Although no one has bothered me sexually, after my jewelry is stolen I no longer feel safe there.

Job Interview

One day Heidi takes me with her to check out a job possibility the houseboat owner told her about. We go to an apartment where, to our surprise, the filming of a porno movie is already in progress. I don't feel comfortable at all. I tell Heidi, "I don't want to stay here."

Heidi doesn't like the setup either, and we soon leave. But, as we're going, a scary looking guy starts following us. We walk as quickly as we can back to the houseboat. I remember feeling very frightened. Heidi and I are lucky that we both get away from this situation safely. Amsterdam's scene at the time is really fluid. It would've been quite easy for a couple of girls from another country to disappear without a trace.

Our whole living situation feels creepier than ever to me, and it now feels that way even to the much more experienced Heidi. She agrees with me that the guy who owns the houseboat isn't a safe person himself. He probably told the porno makers that since we are young and poor, they could take advantage of us.

So, we decide to move out of the houseboat. But, where to go?

The Flycatcher

We stop by Galaxy, hoping to find another place to crash. While there we meet Ugo, a Dutch Jew who survived the Nazi occupation during World War II. Ugo allows girls to live in his apartment. It isn't a sexual thing (at least not overtly so). We just have to clean his place for him.

But, it *is* a rather strange situation. While we girls are cleaning, Ugo sits in a chair and tries to catch flies with a vacuum cleaner(!) A whole bunch of girls who have run away from home live there. After we've cleaned for him, we pretty much sleep the rest of the day. In the evening, we get dressed up and go to Galaxy or Tulipmania.

Heidi keeps large bricks of hashish in Ugo's refrigerator. She regularly reminds me, "I got us housing, so you have to sell the drugs. That's *your* job."

Because she has me standing outdoors on cold winter nights selling hash, Heidi would give me a few hits of heroin. Not too much — just enough that I don't mind doing what she wants me to do. I get hooked on it again, making me even more subject to her control.

Busted

One night after I've been in Holland about 3 months, the police arrest me and everyone else who's dealing drugs on the street. Heidi is inside the club when the arrests take place, but naturally she hears about it. She comes to the police station to see me, and I tell her I'm being deported to Germany. (Although I grew up in Italy, I have German citizenship via my mother.)

From past experience, I know I'm going to be sick from heroin withdrawal. Before I'm taken away, I beg Heidi, "Please give me some heroin. I don't know what's going to happen, and I'm really not well." Heidi has heroin on her, and there are times when we're not being watched. The police aren't going to search me again — because they're getting rid of me. She could give me something to help me get through this, but she doesn't.

The Dutch police put me in a van with 2 men in their 20's who also are being deported to Germany. One of them is a scary guy who belongs to an infamous motorcycle gang. The other guy, like me, is being deported for selling drugs. In general, the Dutch police bring deportees just over the border, rather than to the community they're from. However, since I'm a minor, they bring me to a temporary home for girls once we're in Germany.

Now that I'm at this group home, I'm wondering, *What the hell is going to happen to me?* I'm too sick to sleep, because I'm going through heroin withdrawal. I'm getting increasingly anxious because I have no idea how long I'm going to be locked up. Plus, I'm completely isolated — no one comes to talk to me.

The room is decent enough. At least it doesn't feel like jail did. But still, there are bars over the windows, and I can't leave. After awhile, I go berserk and pull down the curtains and curtain rods, breaking the whole contraption. At this point, I really am nuts.

Soon the authorities find out I've lied about my permanent residence. I told them I live in America (as I'd said when arrested in Munich), because I'm hoping they'll send me back to mother in the US. I tell myself, *Once I'm there, I'll figure out what to do next.*

But, father contacted Interpol after I went missing from Bolzitano, which the police discover as soon as they run my passport number through their system. They contact father, and he comes to the group home to pick me up (again with Petra).

The director of the group house tells father not to take me home to Bolzitano while I'm still sick from heroin withdrawal. Because I've pulled down the curtains and curtain rods, and have basically been acting crazy for some time, she suggests that I instead be taken to a psychiatrist for evaluation. Father is totally skeptical even of family doctors, never mind psychiatrists(!) But, he grudgingly agrees to her recommendation.

𝕽escue 𝕺peration
Examination Room

Father takes me to Dr. Marsh, an internist friend of his in Schwaz, Austria. Dr. Marsh's hair is gray, and he's probably in his 50's or 60's. But, he has a young wife — she can't be more than 25 or 26 — and they've recently had a baby. She's quite beautiful, with long, thick, black hair in a single braid on the side, like a Modigliani painting.

I stay in their apartment for a few days while he's evaluating me. During one visit to his clinic, I'm seated in an exam room waiting for some test results. Dr. Marsh comes into the room, pushes me onto the bed, and starts kissing me. I'm thinking, *Oh my God, this is insane — this man is married, I'm sleeping under the same roof with his young wife and child, and here he is sexually assaulting me!* Fortunately, he doesn't become violent, so I'm able to fight off his advances without great difficulty. But still, it's confusing and very upsetting.

To his credit, Dr. Marsh does have me evaluated by an actual psychiatrist. She, in turn, makes a written recommendation (which I'm able to see later on) that under no circumstances should I live with father again. Only in a different environment will it be possible for me to get off drugs, return to school, and hopefully grow up to be a healthy adult. If I return to father's home instead, she's very concerned that I won't recover.

When father reads this report, he starts shouting, *"Psychiatrists* are crazy! *They* need to be evaluated; *they* need to 'see someone'. *You* don't need a psychiatrist, and *I* don't need a psychiatrist. All you need is to live in the mountains, get fresh air from hiking and climbing, and you'll be *fine!"*

This is father's remedy for *everything*: Eat good food, go hiking, climb mountains, and breathe clean air. That's all.

I think this is good advice in general. When someone has a healthy family, it's great to go hiking with them. But when you have a crazy father who already tries to isolate you from everybody else and make you his prisoner, then the last thing you need is to go hiking in the mountains alone with him.

Franz and Johanna

Again to his credit, Dr. Marsh finds a family in Schwaz for me to live with. To this day, I'm conflicted because some of the same men in my life who've assaulted or abused me sexually have been quite helpful otherwise. Father clearly has abused me, in a number of ways. But, as noted, he's the one person who's always there for me whenever I need him, and he looks out for me the whole time I'm growing up.

Likewise, this physician who can't be trusted to be alone with me, and who has already sexually assaulted me, nevertheless does the right thing in referring me to Franz and Johanna, a young couple who also live in Schwaz. Dr. Marsh knows them both, and thinks they'd be a good match for me.

He gets in touch with them, and they agree to take me in. Franz is an author and about 35. Johanna is maybe 25. I'll be a housekeeper for them, and a nanny for their children. In turn, they'll feed, shelter, and generally look out for me. Father allows this move at first, although he yells about "the stupid doctor", "the stupid psychiatrist", "the stupid report" — on and on. He isn't really on-board with any of it.

Easy Withdrawal

When I first get to Schwaz, I withdraw from heroin for a few more days. But, once I've settled in with Franz, Johanna, and their 2 children, I'm able to stay off heroin without much effort. On weekends, when Franz is home watching the kids, Johanna takes me to the little tea room she owns. She's sort of a hippie, yet also intellectually engaged, as is Franz. So she starts helping me prepare to return to school.

I'm completely comfortable in this arrangement. Johanna and Franz are cool people, and they have a solid marriage. For the 1st time, I feel I'm part of a loving family. I don't have an urge to escape into drugs, as has happened everywhere else. For example, I didn't feel I belonged at mother's house in Arlington. So, I found ways to get drugs, like going to dangerous neighborhoods in DC, and riding around the city with a guy who has a gun in his glove compartment. I had sex with a few such guys, though I had no idea who they were, or where they came from. I didn't care.

Now that I'm with Johanna, Franz, and their kids, I no longer feel I have to put myself at risk to escape from a painful living situation. They like me a lot, and I very much want to stay with them and watch their children. Unfortunately, after I've been living with them for 1 or 2 months, Petra shows up to conduct a look-see(!) Although I do help out with house-cleaning, Johanna and Franz are both very creative, so the place isn't neat and tidy at all times. I can still see Petra standing there. She's about 5' 10" to begin with. In her high heels, she stands over 6'. Her small head atop a tall body makes her look all the more ridiculous in her mink coat and matching mink hat.

She reports to father that the house is a filthy mess, and he should get me out of there ASAP. That's all father has to hear. He arrives the next day and forces me to leave with him. I'm crying, because I want to stay. Franz, Johanna, and their kids also want me to stay. It's a sad day for us, but I don't have the strength to refuse father — I'm still 16.

Before I'm taken away, though, Johanna quietly says to me, "We'll come and get you."

Mountain Getaway

Father soon packs me off to his mountain house in Sulden (which is what he's wanted to do all along). Although I have no love for her, and she strongly dislikes me, father makes Petra my chaperone. During the day, Petra and I ski together. She drinks daily (and also nightly), and on the ski slopes she has a flask filled with either German *schnapps* or Italian *grappa* (both are fruity spirits) in her jacket pocket. She'd give me a flask too. The only way we can tolerate being in each other's company, and the whole situation, is for both of us to get drunk.

I stay in touch with Franz and Johanna. They know I'm being emotionally abused by father and Petra, and that I'm mi-serable living with them. Before long, Johanna calls me and says that she and Franz are coming to rescue me. They've devised a plan: We'll meet on the mountain slope, and ski downhill together. Then, they'll take me with them back to Austria, where they'll go to family court to apply for custody over me.

It's all so remarkable. I hadn't met Franz and Johanna until a few months earlier. Now, because they've taken a liking to me, and because of their compassion, they're willing to risk getting seriously on the wrong side of father, and perhaps the law as well.

As planned, Johanna and Franz show up on the mountaintop where I've been skiing with Petra. And yet, in spite of everything, I can't go through with it. I'm so upset that I start crying. I remember saying to them, "I'm sorry. I can't do this. I have to stay with father — I would be betraying him if I left."

Running away to live with Fabio was different. He was a lover, but in no way a father-figure. And, he was on the other side of town, not in another country. But to run off with Johanna and Franz would be to choose different *parents*. I have to be loyal to father, because he's always been loyal to me.

Afterward, I make the mistake of telling father what has happened. I naively think he will understand the pain I'm in, and be happy that, nonetheless, out of loyalty I've chosen to stay with him. Instead, he's furious. He shouts, "How *dare* they!?" He curses, yells, rants, and raves.

I realize too late that I should have kept my mouth shut and not said anything. I ask myself, *Why didn't I leave? What was I thinking? That this would ever change and get better? That this time would be different?*

A Pointed Question

Petra continues to be my chaperone, until one evening when father is visiting us at the mountain house. He invites both of us out to dinner, but Petra declines, probably because she knows he will pay more attention to me than to her.

As it turns out, dinner with father goes unusually well. We both have a lot to drink, which on this occasion helps us get along.

When we get back to the house, Petra, emerges from the bedroom wearing a long white nightgown, and stands in the doorway. She too has had a lot to drink, while nursing her resentment of me. She asks father, accusingly, "Why don't you *f**** your daughter?!"

Enraged, I charge at her. Petra flees back to the bedroom, jumps into bed, and tries to hide under the covers. I am furiously assaulting her. I think I'd have killed Petra then and there if father hadn't pulled me off of her. (Looking back, however, I realize she *is* onto something: Father and I do have an almost incestuous emotional connection.)

He deals with the conflict between Petra and me by pretending to get rid of her, but actually, just removing her from my sight. What I really want is to be free of him myself. Instead, he makes *her* leave our house. Yet, they continue having an affair, though now they try to hide it. Either he visits her, or he sneaks her into our house. The whole situation remains uncomfortable for all of us.

Capriccio Espagnol

While we're on a skiing trip, Petra and I meet a psychiatrist from Rome. He must be in his late 30's/early 40's, and by now I'm 17. He can't take his eyes off me and, given our age difference, the intensity of his staring is clearly inappropriate. But, he puts me in contact with a family from Rome who own a resort in Spain and need help for the summer season.

Since I don't know what else to do with my life, I accept a summer job at their resort. They hire me because I speak English, German, and Italian; and they have a lot of guests from countries where 1 or more of these languages are spoken. I'm going to be the resort's translator and tourist guide. Fa-ther likes the idea of my getting this hands-on experience, since he wants me to run the hotel he plans on building.

It doesn't work out well, though, because I party too much. I don't take drugs while there, but I drink a lot. And, I develop a crush on the owner of the resort — because I have no idea how to be just a friend with a man. (I think that being raised by father has a lot to do with this.)

I'm deficient in social skills generally. I don't know how to talk and get comfortable, unless I'm high on drugs or I've had a few drinks. Further, my drinking gets progressively worse. I meet 2 German bikers and a girl who are staying at the resort. I go to a bar with them. Later, I wake up in the middle of the night — while they're making a porno movie!

Even before mother left, I was always closer to father.

I wonder to myself, *How did I wind up here?* I keep getting into these crazy situations like drinking myself into a black-out and putting myself at risk sexually. I've completely lost common sense. Or, more accurately, I haven't developed it yet. And, now I'm in trouble with the resort owners (whom I'm living with), because I stayed out the whole night. I'm still 17 and they feel responsible, having assured father they'll look after me.

Eventually, they fire me, and I then fly to Rome. There (for some reason I can no longer recall), I stay with the psychiatrist who got me the job. He's bald with a beard — not someone I'm attracted to. So, when he tries to make a move on me, I find it utterly gross. Fortunately, I succeed at fending him off. (By this time, I'm accustomed to gross men coming on to me.)

Consistent with his plan to build a hotel in the backyard, father soon arranges for me to spend 2 semesters attending a school for hotel management. It turns out to be largely a party school for young people whose families have money. I drink a lot while there, so I learn very little.

After graduating, I move back and forth a few times between living with father and living with Fabio.

𝔐𝔶 1𝔰𝔱 𝔓𝔯𝔢𝔤𝔫𝔞𝔫𝔠𝔶

By November 1977 I've turned 19, and I'm pregnant by Fabio. This isn't an unplanned pregnancy. I want to have Fabio's baby and be his partner for life. I also want to leave Italy and move to Germany. So despite father's repeated, and sometimes violent, attempts to separate us, Fabio's son is now father's grandchild. (If father weren't so adamantly against Fabio, I probably wouldn't have stayed with him, because even back then I realize that Fabio isn't going anywhere in life.)

Now that I'm pregnant, I completely change my lifestyle. I stop using heroin, and I stop smoking cigarettes, pot, and hash. I want to have a family, to make a home with Fabio, and to have peace and quiet. Fabio is the kind of quiet man whom I (naively) envision will be a good father. I do not consider getting married because, as mentioned earlier, I promised myself that I'd never marry — I've never dreamt about the white dress and the rest. But, I do want to live with Fabio for the rest of our days (or so I feel at the time).

And yet, at 5 months pregnant, I'm back living with father.

One day we're having lunch together with Thea, father's secretary. He surprises me with the news that he's planning on redecorating my room. He probably thinks it's an inducement for me to continue living with him after my child is born. However, for years he promised me my own room, but wouldn't let me have one — until Petra started sleeping in his bed. Now that I intend to live with Fabio, there's no reason to redecorate my room.

I look at father and say, "I think it's a little too late for that. The room should have been redecorated when I was 6, not now that I'm 19."

Father is so furious at my jibe that he tosses a glass of wine at me. I jump up from the table and try to run away. He then throws me down the stairs. I manage to flee from the house. It's the last time I see father until sometime after my baby is born.

Return Engagement

Around this time, mother's marriage to Knut is on the rocks. She's found out he's been having an affair with her best friend. (Later, she'll forgive her friend, but not Knut.) However, because she doesn't have a career, her financial options are limited. Father pays her expenses to come to Bolzitano to explore the possibility of a reconciliation. (Petra gets shunted to the sideline while mother is visiting.)

Although mother sleeps beside him during her visit, apparently she refuses him physical intimacy, because later she mirthfully tells me that he placed a carrot on her mattress as a substitute for him.

Baby Clothes

The clothes I wore as a baby are still in the room I had before mother left. She'd saved them, and father hasn't touched anything in the room since her departure. It's almost like a mausoleum. When I'm a child, it's a strange but fascinating room for me to visit. Entering it requires climbing a couple of steps. There's a loft bed, with a gate in front of it, as if I were behind a cage when I was a baby. There's a combination closet and dresser against one wall. As a child, I'd go through the drawers looking at all my baby clothes that mother left there — little slippers, socks, shirts, and baby rompers.

In a gesture I'm grateful for, during her visit mother washes and irons all my old baby clothes, packs them into a suitcase, and brings the suitcase to where I'm staying with Fabio (all without father's knowledge).

But, her visit has a certain dreamlike quality for me. She's back for a few days — then she's gone.

Appointment in Berlin

There's nothing keeping me in Bolzitano. Even though I love him, life with father has been unbearable ever since mother left. As for the rest of the town, it's been a scandal all along that I'm partnered with the notorious Fabio. Worse yet, from their point of view, I'm now pregnant with his baby — but I still have no intention of marrying him.

After father throws me down the stairs, I decide to have my baby in Berlin. Somehow it feels right. As noted earlier, Berlin is the birthplace of mother and her ancestors. Having been born there myself, I'm a German citizen. So, from a practical standpoint, I'm entitled to Germany's relatively generous welfare benefits for a single mother.

I'm still 5 months pregnant when we set out for Berlin — with no money, no insurance, and no place to stay. Just a suitcase filled with my old baby clothes. Although I've stopped using drugs, Fabio hasn't. He has no job, nor any ambition to get one. Looking back, I realize the whole thing is crazy.

I don't remember exactly how we get by in the beginning. Maybe we stay in a hotel for a few days. Soon, though, we find a 4th-floor walk-up in a building that's scheduled to be demolished by the city. The landlord is not supposed to be letting out the apartments, so the rent is really cheap.

There are maybe 20 apartments in all but, besides ours, only 2 or 3 are occupied. Building repairs aren't being made any longer, so the place is falling apart. Some of the hallway windows are broken, and birds are nesting in nooks — when they aren't flying about. It's all kind of eerie.

Medical Emergency

Before long my water breaks, because I'm under so much stress — all those years of fearing father, combined with now being pregnant and not having any money or stability. Not having anything, really. Plus, I'm in Berlin, a huge change from a small town, and I'm intimidated by the big city. Fabio is too high on drugs to be of any help. I'm completely desperate. An ambulance takes me to a nearby hospital. I'm terrified that my baby is going to die. Fortunately, the doctors succeed in stabilizing my pregnancy.

Alone

During the 6 weeks I'm in the hospital, I'm not allowed out of bed. The doctors fear that if I'm up and about, my baby may be born too prematurely to survive. I have no one to talk to except the doctors and nurses. Though they're very nice, they are too busy to keep me company.

I remember meditating a lot while I'm in the hospital. When I was 16, Fabio and I attempted to get off heroin by joining a program called Transcendental Meditation. (It was quite trendy in the 1970's.) We were taught how to meditate, and were given a mantra. Meditating every day helps me get through the 6-week hospital stay.

My newborn, Lukas, is 2 months premature, but otherwise healthy. However, it's just the 2 of us. No family members are present — neither father, nor mother. Not even Fabio (who is back in Italy, doing drugs). No visitors, cards, or gifts — no anyone or anything. It's a very lonely time in my life.

From today's vantage point, I realize that typically a mother is present for her daughter's pregnancy, particularly the 1st one. But, mother hasn't been present for me since I was 5. And so, during my pregnancy and when I give birth, it doesn't seem to me unusual that mother isn't there. At that time, such thoughts would have been much too painful to dwell on, but I now realize that I especially needed her then.

Losing Respect

When Fabio returns to Berlin, the 3 of us live in the same rundown building for a while longer. It's obviously an unsuitable place for raising a newborn. I have to carry the baby carriage, groceries, *etc*, up and down 4 flights — while avoiding the stairs that are broken. I remember making tea and heating food, so we do have gas. But, we don't have hot water from the tap. I have to heat water on the stove just to bathe Lukas. After a time, though, the welfare office gives us a better apartment.

As it happens, the owner of the building we've just left also owns a bed-and-breakfast. He hires me to be its maid, which I had experience doing for father's bed-and-breakfast. The pay for being a part-time maid isn't much of course, but it's a helpful addition to the welfare benefits.

Fabio helps somewhat, but isn't really that supportive. He does love Lukas, and watches him while I'm at work. The 2 of them are quite close. So, in terms of giving Lukas love and attention, Fabio isn't a bad father. But, instead of getting a job himself, he finds a local doctor who prescribes him more narcotics. I don't know exactly what Fabio is taking, but I can tell he's using. I'm the one who has to do all of the everyday things necessary to support and run a household of 2 adults and a baby.

I'm finally losing respect for Fabio. I've been hoping he'd man-up and get a job once our son is born. But, he doesn't. He's an addict, and drugs are his only real priority. Even while I'm pregnant, he doesn't stop using. I think that this is pretty selfish on his part, because I'm not the only one who has a son — Fabio does too.

The Boys in Brazil

As with Canada and the US, Latin American countries are very ethnically diverse. In the years immediately following WW II, the already existing German and Italian ethnic enclaves in a number of Latin American countries help smooth the path to resettlement for newcomers from Germany and Italy — regardless of their past.

Many immigrants are looking for job opportunities unavailable in war-torn Europe. But, some of them are also seeking to escape responsibility for war crimes. Ironically, although a number of war criminals find sanctuary in Argentina, there are also some 45,000 European Jews who emigrate there after WW II. Many people simply want the war to be over, and to move on with their life.

Yet, for surviving civilians and soldiers alike, it's not easy to get over the events of WW II, particularly if they occurred during one's youth. And so, in 1979 father joins a dozen or so wartime comrades from Germany and Austria, and together they travel to Latin America — specifically Argentina, Brazil, Paraguay, and Uruguay — to meet up with other veterans of the war. Mother calls it a "Nazi reunion".

After he returns from Latin America, father swears that it's the best trip of his life. It turns out that he has less than a year to live. While he's dying in the hospital (of liver cirrhosis), he recalls fondly that he and his buddies had already consumed the airliner's supply of alcohol before it had left airspace over Africa.

The doctors may have already told him before the trip that his liver condition is terminal. I wouldn't be surprised if father were the one who organizes the whole expedition.

𝕯𝖎𝖊 𝕯ä𝖒𝖒𝖊𝖗𝖚𝖓𝖌

A few months after the reunion in Latin America, my cousin Astrid calls (I'm still in Berlin at the time), and tells me that father is gravely ill. His skin and eyes have turned yellow, and he's been diagnosed with cirrhosis of the liver. He wants me to come home to Bolzitano. Father has always stood by me in my times of need. I can't refuse to be by his side now that he's dying.

I pack and take Lukas with me back to Bolzitano (leaving Johan with Fabio in Berlin). Though father has been admitted to the local hospital, it's just a general healthcare facility, so the doctors advise that he be moved to Sterzing, because the hospital there has a dedicated liver clinic.

I visit father a couple of times a week. (Driving to Sterzing over Alpine mountain roads takes almost 2 hours each way.) I feel a great deal of distress watching him lying in a hospital bed, gradually getting weaker. And so, I relapse on heroin. At first I use just a little bit. But, as his condition worsens, so does my habit.

During one hospital visit I learn that Ariel, an ex-girlfriend of father's, has suddenly shown up. In the early 1960's, she was a pretty famous fashion model in Europe. Sometime in the late 60's, she became father's girlfriend. More than a decade later, now that father is sick and dying, Ariel is back. And, father wants me to take the equivalent of $10,000 out of his home safe.

I ask him, "Why do you want $10,000?"

He answers, "I owe Ariel money — I have to repay her."

I lose it with father. In the past, I've never had the courage to push back. But, I feel I need to protect him, because he's increasingly delusional. For example, in spite of being permanently bedridden, he wants to buy a brand new Mercedes — and a BMW motorcycle! And now, he wants to give $10,000 to this woman who I'm sure has taken advantage of his generosity in the past.

In the end, it's my decision. I tell father, "I'm not giving Ariel *any* money. She's lying! You don't owe her anything, and I don't want to see her in this hospital again."

When Ariel comes to the hospital while I'm there, I confront her, "Why are you suddenly back now that father is dying — if not to financially exploit him?" I tell her to go to hell. (That's the last we see of her.)

It feels so strange. For the first time in my life, *I* need to protect *him*. I'm not afraid of him anymore, because I know he's losing his physical strength and his psychological power.

But now I fear for my own future, because I've never known anyone else I could always count on. As the reality sets in that father is going to die, I begin to wonder, *What am I to do? I certainly am not ready to stand on my own 2 feet. And now, I am using heroin again.* A part of me knows that I'm not well. But the only way for me to cope with watching father's steadily deteriorating condition is to 'self-medicate', to numb myself with heroin throughout the whole death watch.

As his physical health declines, so does his mental health. For example, I have a photo of Lukas and me enlarged to poster size, and place it on a wall near his bed. On my next visit, I find he has torn apart the poster and thrown the shreds on the floor (perhaps because Fabio is Lukas's father). The nurses tell me that he gets very angry and has fits. Sometimes they have to put him in physical restraints, because he can get dangerous — even for the hospital staff.

Plus, father wants to stray far from his bed — to drive away in his (imaginary) new Mercedes Benz or else on his (equally imaginary) BMW motorcycle. He tells the nurses his Mercedes is outside, and his friends are waiting for him. So, his mind is deteriorating along with his body.

Eventually, the doctors tell me that there's nothing more they can do to help him. I take father home to Bolzitano in March or April 1980. I'm then on-call for father 24/7, even if merely for a glass of water. I hire Letta, a nurse-therapist, to help care for him. Letta is quite energetic, and I feel guilty that she's doing so much more than I am for father. (Later, I find out that she's popping pills. It's no wonder she has so much energy!)

On one occasion, father lunges at me with a kitchen knife in his hand. But before reaching me, he falls to the floor. It's a great relief to see father "de-fanged", because I've been so afraid of him my whole life. And yet, I also still love him. To see him lose his power is heart-rending. Part of me is happy that he's losing his power and strength, but part of me is absolutely depressed — and terrified.

Father dies in May of 1980, at age 60. I've never had to make funeral arrangements, and at this moment I'm completely numb. His secretary, Thea, insists that *she* is going to dress him — in one of his expensive hand-tailored business suits. I'm thinking, *However you want to dress him, whether in his pajamas or a suit, that truly doesn't matter to me now*.

However, though I'm not sure why, I don't want an open casket. Whatever the underlying reason, I know I don't want people to stand there looking at him. I decide it'll be a closed-casket funeral — whether other people like it or not.

He Stopped Loving Her Today

She came to see him one last time;
We all wondered if she would.
And it kept runnin' through my mind...
***This time,* he's over her for good.** (Braddock, Putnam)

In spite of everything, mother comes from America to father's funeral. She spends some time with the boys and me, and then goes back to her life there.

Heroin: The Downward Spiral

After father dies, all restraints are off. I use heroin for another 3 years — with calamitous results.

Still only 21, and addicted once again, I inherit father's entire estate, which includes an agricultural equipment manufacturing company; the bed-and-breakfast; a commercial building with cash-paying tenants (such as the gas station and restaurant where my parents met); a mountain house; the apartment he raised me in and adjoining apartments; a large plot of land including a fruit grove, swimming pool, and sauna; 3 cars; and a number of valuable antiques and paintings.

Though my inheritance is worth a few million in today's dollars, in under 3 years the money is gone — due to my heroin habit, and "friends of the family" who take advantage of my vulnerability.

Designer Apartment

Continuing to live in father's apartment would feel much too painful, because there's so much unresolved hurt from the past. Every time I'm in it, I start shaking and feeling faint. I know we can't live there.

Besides the several apartments in Bolzitano, father leaves me 2 apartments in Neumarkt, a little town about 15 minutes away. (I think father grew up there.) The 2 apartments are adjacent to each other. One is a studio, the other a 1 bedroom. I decide to break through the walls and make a single large apartment. The studio apartment becomes the living room of the combined space, and Lukas gets his own bedroom. We now have a really great space to live in.

Mother hasn't yet left. We go shopping together at Steiner's, one of the most expensive furniture stores in the region. (Although I'm a heroin addict who can barely keep her eyes open, mother is all excited because she's going shopping.)

We pick out "designer" everything — a perfect kitchen, beautiful carpets for the living room, new curtains, even an elaborate chandelier. Fabio and I get ourselves a bedroom set, with a wicker bed and beautiful Danish-wood closets. We have 2 bathrooms and 2 balconies. Everything is custom-fit to the dimensions of our apartment. It's awesome — like one of those apartments featured in a glossy magazine.

Rounding off my shopping spree, I buy 2 hi-speed Citroën sedans — 1 for Fabio and 1 for myself. In total, I spend tens of thousands of dollars, all in cash — and all with mother's encouragement.

Mother is so happy that I have a gorgeous apartment. But, like the time the heroin spoon and syringe fell out of my boot in front of her, she continues to pretend to be blind to my addiction. (Sometime later, she will change dramatically.)

Realizing that I'm not able to handle all these new responsibilities, I beg mother, "Please, stay and help me. I have all these businesses. I'm supposed to know what to do, but I have no idea — and I don't trust Thea. Also, I want to open a health food store, and I need help. Father's apartment in Bolzitano is now empty. I'll give you his apartment or the new apartment in Neumarkt — whichever one you want."

But, mother insists on returning to America. To be fair, she never was accepted by the locals in Bolzitano. And, I'm sure she doesn't want to be gossiped about as a gold-digger who left father while he was still alive, but returns to live off her daughter's inheritance from him now that he's dead. By contrast, she loves living in America. The very things that some Europeans disdain, like shopping malls and the consumer culture in general, are what she seems to like most.

Plus, her marriage to Knut has ended, and Kim is still only 7. Mother needs to get on with managing her own life, rather than trying to rescue me from my irresponsibility.

As luck would have it, on her flight back to America she is seated beside Rod, a successful businessman. Rod is a widower, an alcoholic, and a highly promiscuous womanizer with 3 adult children. But he has money and his own company (like father did). He soon becomes mother's 3rd husband.

Maybe she views this marriage as a way to avoid winding up old and poor in America — something she greatly fears. She and Kim move from Knut's home in upscale Reston, Virginia to Rod's home in more modest Easton, Maryland.

Fire Hazard

Meanwhile, I'm in South Tyrol in our beautiful new apartment with our brand new expensive furniture, which I'm constantly burning with cigarettes. Because junkies often nod out while smoking — and I'm smoking like a chimney — there are burn marks on the carpet, on the surface of the tables, on the nightstand, and on my clothing.

Nodding out with a cigarette in my hand sometimes causes little fires. Usually, I wake up on my own in time to put them out. One time, however, it's 3-year-old Lukas who wakes up and smells smoke from my comforter, half of which is already ablaze. I put out the fire, tell Lukas he is my hero, and then we both go back to sleep — as if nothing unusual happened.

In Fair Verona

Verona, Italy is the setting of world literature's most famous tragic love story: *Romeo and Juliet*. I drive there from South Tyrol as often as once a week. But, I'm not on a rendezvous with a human Romeo. My Veronese lover is heroin. Whenever it isn't available in Bolzitano, Verona is the nearest city large enough to have a steady supply. When my withdrawal is so severe that I need to make this trip, I'm in a big hurry to get there. I put the pedal to the metal, reaching my Citroën's maximum speed of 150 mph. Sometimes I leave Lukas with a babysitter. At other times, he rides in the car with me.

On one occasion, I sideswipe a much slower moving Fiat 500, causing it to flip onto its side. But I just continue on my way to Verona. I need heroin; there's no time to stop. However, after I've shot up in Verona, I feel well enough to pull over at the scene of the accident on the return trip and admit my fault. I'm very relieved to learn that miraculously no one's been hurt. (It's probably the reason the police just let me go.)

Another time, I set out late one evening for Merano — which is smaller than Verona, but much closer. My withdrawal is already so bad that I take Roipnol to calm my nerves. (Roipnol is actually a sleeping pill. It's sometimes used as a date-rape drug.) I wake up in the middle of the night in an open field — not knowing how I got there. The car won't move, because a wheel has fallen off! Though not really knowing where I am, I somehow manage to walk home. (Fortunately, Lukas isn't with me on this trip.)

Back to Bolzitano

Johan, our 2nd son (also planned), arrives in February of 1982, almost 2 years after father's death. Because I now have money, I can easily afford another child, so there isn't the drama that attended my pregnancy with Lukas.

Now that we have 2 sons, I decide to move back to Bolzitano into father's old apartment. Enough time has passed that the emotional turmoil I once felt when there is now manageable. It seems ridiculous that it's been sitting empty for 2 years. In the Bolzitano apartment, the boys will grow up having access to a spacious backyard, a large swimming pool, a sauna, and other amenities.

We fill the Bolzitano apartment with the expensive furnishings from Neumarkt. They were custom-built, so they no longer fit just right. But, they still look fine (in spite of the cigarette burns).

Because I'm still using heroin, my circumstances continue to worsen. I forget to leave open a faucet to let a little water run through the pipes in the mountain house in Sulden. When winter comes, the pipes freeze and burst. Mother arrives on an inspection tour later that year (no longer pretending to be unaware of my addiction), and finds the house has water damage everywhere.

I tell the restaurant owner who's renting space in my building that instead of paying monthly rent, she can give me $200 or $300 every day, and after a time she'll own the space outright. Basically, I sell the space for peanuts. I don't recall whether we even have a written contract.

I buy gas on credit every day from the man who rents the gas station. At the end of the month, instead of him paying *me* rent, I'm in debt to *him*.

The Big Giveaway

While father is still in the hospital dying of cirrhosis, one of my cousins comes to me and says, "Since you don't know anything about your father's farm equipment business, you should consider giving a part of the business to Thea and father's 3 other main workers. They've all been with your father 20+ years, and have always been loyal."

My cousin proposes I give them a minority interest in the business. They'll work harder, because they'll get a percentage of the profits. But, I'll still have a majority interest.

I reply, "Sure." If someone wants to sleep with me, or even to take my soul, it doesn't matter anymore. At this point, I'm so heavily addicted to heroin that I'd have given away my left leg as long as I have my drugs. So, *Yes, of course, I'll give away almost half of the business,* is my attitude.

Thea has long been the overseer of all of father's business affairs. By the time I'm a teenager, I'm rarely home, so she'd cook lunch and dinner for father. This is why she's present at lunch when father says he'll redecorate my room (but then throws me down the stairs).

My sense is that whenever father didn't have another girlfriend, he grew closer to Thea. When he did have a substitute, Thea would get shelved. Although he did buy her fine jewelry and other expensive gifts, I feel that she's resentful that she never became father's wife. She's the one woman who tolerated father's nonsense the whole time. She probably took care of him in various ways, and suffered a lot.

Now that father's gone, Thea is running the agricultural equipment company. The 3 men who also have an ownership interest are merely her puppets. They're good helpers, but she's the boss.

Thea doesn't cook just food. As father's secretary for many years, she's excellent at cooking the books too. Initially, I'm getting about $15,000 from the business every month. But, little by little, the steady stream of income becomes a trickle, since Thea knows I'm going down the tubes. By 1982, I'm not getting any money at all from the manufacturing business.

There's no money from the restaurant either at the end of the month, because I've been taking it out daily to spend on narcotics. Nor is there cash from the gas station, since Fabio and I both fill up our cars there. The mountain house is kaput, and I sell the apartment in Neumarkt, almost giving it away.

Yet, in spite of everything sliding downhill, I decide to open a health food store! This may seem ironic, considering how unhealthily Fabio and I are living. But, there's a part of me that does want to get better.

I take a class and pass the required exam to get a license to sell health food. Ludwiga, a friend of father, owns a building with a boutique in front. She wants to sell the store space in back. I borrow $100,000 from a bank in order to buy the store, because I have so little cash on hand. However, Ludwiga doesn't give me a key to the store, and due to my addiction, I don't even ask her for one. The business never opens.

Double-Cross

Fabio keeps pestering me to quit heroin. This too may seem ironic, since he's using also. Plus, he got me started (admittedly, only at my urging, after he hesitated a good deal). But, my habit is much worse than his. If there's no heroin to be had, he's okay with having a few drinks, taking a Roipnol, and going to sleep. By contrast, I *have to* have heroin. (Thus, the mad dashes to Verona.)

By the summer of 1982, I agree to go on a trip with him so we both can get clean. We won't be around familiar surroundings, which can trigger drug cravings. And we'll have the novelty of a new place to distract us from these urges when they do arise. We won't take any drugs with us — we'll go cold turkey. We journey to the island of Elba off the coast of Tuscany. In the vocabulary of 12-Step programs such as Alcoholics Anonymous and Narcotics Anonymous (about which, more to come), we're "going on a geographic".

I invite my cousin Astrid to come with us, in part because she can help babysit Lukas, as well as help with our newest member of the family, Johan, who is then only a few months old. Another reason is that I want to find out what is going on between Astrid and Fabio.

Since our little family has been back in Bolzitano, I've noticed she's been visiting us quite often. And she seems overly familiar with Fabio. When I tell him I invited her, he asks peevishly, "Do we have to bring *her?*"

Soon after we arrive in Elba, I get the surprise of my life. Returning from a trip to town one day, I find Astrid and Fabio in bed together — with 4-year-old Lukas in between them! I immediately gather up my sons and return to Bolzitano (and heroin), leaving Astrid and Fabio behind.

I'm heartbroken that Fabio is having an affair with Astrid — the cousin I've always felt is like a sister. This is something I can't just "get over". Everything else is already bad. Father has died, I'm unable to manage without him, and I'm still using heroin.

But Fabio's affair with Astrid is the end of the world. He's the only man I've ever loved completely. I thought he loved me in return. We've been using drugs together; we've had 2 sons together; we've been trying to get clean together. I thought he'd be at my side to the end of our days. The fact that he's betrayed me with *Astrid* is what's most painful.

Fabio doesn't get a chance to say goodbye to his sons or me. By the time he awakens from his drugged stupor, we're gone. When he returns to Bolzitano, he claims that it's Astrid who kept hitting on him, which is why he tried to discourage me from bringing her to Elba with us. But, it's not as if he were helpless to resist. I make him move out.

After this turn of events, I can no longer cope with anything. I leave father's old apartment, and move into a nearby hotel with Lukas and Johan. I'm now on a virtual suicide mission with heroin.

Fabio in Later Years

I visit Fabio, in the trailer park he lives in, during a trip to Europe in 1992. (I've settled in the US by then.) He tells me he was arrested by the Italian authorities in the mid-1980's. I know the police had wanted him for a long time. Though he'd been arrested before this, law enforcement hadn't been able to pin anything on him. Fabio is too slick — the kind of under-the-radar drug dealer who's hard to actually convict.

If Fabio is to be believed, he wasn't charged with a specific crime, other than being told his "lifestyle" was considered harmful to society. There was no trial. The authorities just seized his passport and the rest of his possessions, and imprisoned him on a farm on the Island of Sardinia.

They had him herd sheep for 2 or 3 years, in virtual isolation. Because he had no one to talk to, he became almost mute while imprisoned. His biggest fear was that if he died there, no one on the outside would know. In essence, he was "disappeared" by the Italian government.

The one person he had any contact with was a psychotherapist in Austria. He says it was her letters that kept him alive. (So, he did get mail.) Other than his correspondence with her, he was completely isolated.

After prison, he moved to Austria, where he entered rehab and lived in a therapeutic community for awhile. When I visit him again, in 2003, I bring our sons, who by this time are young adults. Now that he's in his late 40's, Fabio's long hair is graying, but he's still quite handsome and charismatic. He has another son, who is probably 5 or 6 years old at the time, but Fabio doesn't live with this son either.

I'm disappointed that Fabio hasn't made more of an effort to stay in touch with our own sons. He's never helped in all these years. No child support at all. Every once in a while, he'd send a letter, but that's it.

Earlier I wrote that when I'm 14, father breaks Fabio's nose the 1st time they meet. I didn't mention that Fabio previously had asked me for the key to the mountain house in Sulden. Just as I won't have a voice of my own to say *no* to Heidi in Amsterdam 2 years later, likewise I'm unable to say *no* to Fabio when I'm 14. He uses the key, with his accomplices, to burglarize the Sulden house and steal valuable paintings by the modernist artist Hans Ebensperger (a personal friend of father). There isn't sufficient evidence to prosecute them, but everyone in town knows they did it, because they've been burglarizing homes for some time. So, father breaking Fabio's nose is a sort of rough justice.

Something else I haven't mentioned is that after father dies, I take a gold tie clip of his to a jeweler to have the clasp removed and the rest fashioned into a pendant that I attach to a necklace. One summer day, Fabio and I are sunning in the backyard in Sulden. To avoid having tan lines, I leave the chain on my chair. When I get back from going inside for a bit, the necklace is gone. I ask Fabio about it, and he says that I must have lost it. But, I know that he stole it.

The house in Sulden. In the middle of winter there's so much snow that I can safely jump off the balcony into it.

Notwithstanding everything that's happened between us, Fabio is still the father of our sons. So, when he joins Facebook a few years ago, we all become Facebook friends. But, Fabio ignores Lukas's birthday; not even posting the words "happy birthday". I realize that during his stay in a Sardinian work camp, he couldn't be expected to send Lukas or Johan a birthday greeting. But on Facebook there's a birthday reminder for each friend, on the day it occurs. If Fabio still cannot bother to acknowledge our son's birthday, I don't see a point to keeping in touch. I tell him I'm very disappointed in him, that he has nothing to bring to the table, and he's just wasting my time. I block him on Facebook and haven't communicated with him since.

Thirty-six years (and 2 grown sons) after I first sat next to Fabio in Café Odeon, this is how it ends. Today, I don't know where he's living or what he's doing. I don't care anymore. I'm sure I'd have heard from mutual acquaintances if he'd died, so I do know that he's still alive — but, that's it.

Summing up: Fabio is the one great love of my life. I was sure I wanted to stay with him for the rest of our days. But, as so often happens with the hopes and dreams of youth, every-thing has turned out quite differently.

Fabio in father's kitchen, sometime after father died.

Astrid in Later Years

As noted earlier, Astrid is diagnosed as bipolar at age 18. She attempts suicide several times before she's 30. Because of a personal tragedy (details in Book II), at age 37 she jumps off the balcony of her 6th story apartment. She survives, but her ankles and feet are broken, and her hips are shattered. Some of her internal organs are severely injured, and she spends the rest of her life severely disabled — mentally and physically — living in mental hospitals and group homes.

After many operations, she dies in September 2008, at age 52. As mentioned, Astrid was like an older sister to me — the one truly empathetic witness to the daily terror I endured while living with father. Perhaps in some way she too was abused by my father — I will never know for sure. As if there were not enough ironies already, Astrid and father are buried in the same grave in a little church cemetery in Bolzitano.

RIP, my dear cousin.

Astrid and I, when we were still so young.

Mother's Intervention

Returning to 1982: Father's death 2 years earlier, and more recently Fabio's betrayal, have pushed me over the edge. My life is now really spinning out of control. Having moved out of father's apartment once again, and overdrawn my bank account, there are times when I sleep in the car with my sons. I've made a huge knot of everything, and I don't know how to untangle it. Up to this point, I've been killing myself in slow motion with drugs. But now my descent is accelerating.

Mother pays a surprise visit to Bolzitano a little before Christmas. Someone must have contacted her with the news that I'm in really bad shape — and therefore her grandsons are imperiled. When mother arrives, she doesn't understand why I don't live in father's apartment, why I'm living in a hotel with the boys, why Fabio is now living with Astrid, and why all the money is gone.

No longer pretending to be unaware of my addiction, mother departs Bolzitano for Rimini, which is on the Adriatic coast a few hundred miles away. There she retains Romano, a lawyer who was a boyfriend of hers before her marriage to father. Romano obtains a court order making him my legal guardian and the custodian of what's left of my estate. The court grants mother custody of Johan and Lukas. During this interval, she also gets passports for them, so she can take them with her to America. (In other words, a lot of effort and expense on her part.)

Since Romano is not a Bolzitano lawyer, he takes no action to redress my rights against the people who have taken advantage of me there. Years later, a savvy local lawyer tells me I could've recovered a lot of the money I lost to the bank. If I wasn't competent to care for my own sons, I surely wasn't competent to take out the bank loan — and this should have been apparent to the bank when they lent the money. But, by the time I learn this, the period for doing anything about it has long since passed. And, in fairness to mother, it's not as if she were given an instruction manual on the best way to rescue her grandsons from her heroin-addicted daughter.

Hitting Bottom

When she returns from Rimini in February, mother informs me she's taking Johan and Lukas to the United States. If I want help, she'll allow me to stay with her while I get treatment. But, she won't let me fly on the same plane with them, because I haven't been honest with her about my drug abuse. She doesn't believe me that I will suddenly stop using, and she fears I'll take drugs on the plane with me.

As mentioned, father would sometimes shout at me, "You should have been in *Russia* — then you'd know how *hard* life is!" At this moment, in my heart I feel like I'm in the coldest place in Siberia.

The next day I follow mother and my sons to America. I have little left to bring with me. I've already sold the antique furniture father collected. He also amassed trunks of smaller antiques from the 1600's and the 1700's. His friends, and some of my own cousins, have been glad to buy them from me for a pittance compared with what they're actually worth. I leave behind all the beautiful, expensive possessions that remain: my car, my furniture, my everything else.

I remember exiting from father's house for the last time, descending the stairs carrying a VCR player and a small TV. (There's nothing else I can quickly barter for heroin.)

On my way to the airport, I trade the VCR player and the TV for one last 1-ounce bag of heroin (just what mother feared I'd do). I think I now have $25 in cash, maybe even less — all that's left of father's estate, which was once worth millions.

I'm leaving the rest behind: residential and commercial buildings, plots of land, businesses, contracts I've signed, and all my other messes. I've lost my father, I've lost everything he spent his life working for, I've lost my sons to a mother I hardly know, I've lost their father and my closest cousin, and I'm now losing my homeland.

I've finally hit bottom.

Coming to America 2

When my flight lands the next day, no one is at the airport to pick me up. I call mother. She explains that because I'm not trustworthy, she's been waiting to see if I'd actually arrive. After the phone call, she does come and get me.

I'm now living on Chesapeake Bay in Easton, Maryland with mother, Rod, and my sister, Kim, who by then is 9 years old. Lukas is 5, and Johan has just turned 1. I have an 8th grade education, no green card, and although I spoke English for the 11 months that I lived in America 9 years earlier, my English is no longer fluent.

In my bedroom in Easton, I heat up a spoon of the last of the 1-ounce bag of heroin I brought with me on the plane. But, I accidentally spill the liquid onto my blanket. I put water on that spot to try to squeeze the heroin out, but it's not recoverable. I feel total despair.

Mother treats me like a prisoner. I'm not allowed to use the car, because I might drive somewhere to score drugs. And though I'm 24 years old with 2 children, she puts rules on the refrigerator for me as if I were still a child myself — what I'm allowed, and not allowed, to do. But, I realize that I've wrecked my life, and she's doing her best to rescue me. Understandably, she resents me for having squandered all of father's money, and now being an economic burden on *her*. And, although she loves them, she doesn't really want the day-to-day responsibility of raising my sons.

Rapid Detox

Though mother won't allow me to use her car, to her credit she drives me to a methadone clinic in Salisbury every day — about an hour's drive from Easton. The clinic rapidly detoxes me, taking just 3 weeks. (In Italy, I was on prescription methadone for 3 years, and I supplemented the methadone with heroin.) Rapid detox has the advantage of reducing the amount of time that withdrawal symptoms linger, and hopefully reduces the time it takes to get back to a normal life.

And so, I'm now withdrawing from both heroin and methadone in mother's kitchen in Easton. Because I can't sleep, I have no energy, so I can't do much of anything. I'm feeling ghastly, like I'm 120 years old — and having a really bad day.

Pneumonia

Rod has a son, Tommy, who's 28 or 29 at the time. He's a hippie like me, and he regularly drives his pickup truck to Florida to sell plants on the side of one or another of the highways there. Mother and Rod think I should help Tommy peddle plants as a 1st step in returning to independence.

I lose track of how long I'm in Florida, because I'm in a virtual fog. I remember just bits and pieces. My immune system is so weak from years of addiction and poor nutrition that I contract pneumonia while there. I'm in really bad shape. I sit up all night, coughing my lungs out, almost unable to breathe. I'm basically dying. Eventually Tommy says, "You better return to Maryland. You need to take care of yourself — and your children."

Predatory Stepfather

Once I'm back in Easton, Rod resumes being friendly but proper — whenever mother is around. However, when she's elsewhere, Rod becomes sexually predatory. He tries to ply me with liquor, saying things like, "I've brought you some rum, because it will help with the withdrawal." After mother has gone to bed, he walks about with his zipper open and his erect penis sticking out of his pants, while I'm sitting in the kitchen suffering through detox. Mother appears not to know about Rod's harassment (as with my heroin use before I hit bottom). But, I feel she must know. What woman wouldn't know this is going on under her own roof?

Looking back, I feel he was sexually violating me whenever he did this (which was almost every night). Once again, I was living with a predatory father-figure. At the time, however, I'm too psychologically broken to feel disgusted, or even upset. In fact, I'm barely feeling anything at all.

I don't say anything about this to mother. She knows my father was sexually inappropriate, and she had reason to strongly suspect that he was doing things to me that are wrong. As already discussed, he sent her pictures of me posing naked. Yet she totally ignored this. I think that any mother should have confronted such a father and demanded to know, *What were you doing? And, why are you sending me these pictures?* Instead, she just puts the pictures in a box.

Rape

Although Rod is dangerous, enduring him is a necessary evil, because he, rather than mother, was dutifully looking after Johan and Lukas when I was in Florida with Tommy.

Now that I'm back in Easton, but still withdrawing from narcotics, Rod resumes his nightly sexual harassment. Soon, he announces that we're all going on a trip to sunny Florida (even though I've just returned). He plans it so that mother will drive down with Lukas and Kim. A day later, Johan and I will take a train. Then Rod will fly there.

Rod arranges things so that after the others have gone, Johan and I will be left with him for 1 night. (Johan is then 13 or 14 months old.) When that evening rolls around, Rod plies me with so much alcohol that I have no physical strength. Plus, I'm already emotionally bankrupt from withdrawal. At some point, I wake up lying on the floor — with Rod on top of me. I'm thinking, *Oh my God, this is horrible! I'm drunk, in and out of a blackout, and this man who is supposed to be my stepfather is on top of me. And yet, mother and my boys are living under this man's roof. What can I do — without jeopardizing my family?*

It's a nightmare that I don't know how to wake up from. The next day, the 3 of us travel to Florida as planned. I'm not sure what, if anything, to do about Rod's having raped me. I don't even hate him for it. I've grown up feeling violated almost daily. Abuse feels normal. I push what Rod did out of my thoughts, and life goes on as before.

On my 1st day there, we all go to the beach. I've never sunbathed under the Florida sun, so I don't know that I need to wear sun screen. I end up terribly sunburned, with blisters all over my chest, a fever, and difficulty falling asleep. It's Rod, not mother, who takes care of me while I am recovering.

I never say a word to mother about being raped by Rod that night. Several years later, she divorces him because he's been sleeping with the maid. After they're divorced, she asks me, "Did Rod ever do anything to you?"

I look at her and reply, "Why would you even think that?" I don't tell her the truth, because she's always wanted to be unaware of anything awkward or unpleasant to the extent possible. So, I let her remain that way.

I couldn't stay angry with father, because he always took care of me, no matter what. Similarly, I can't stay too angry with Rod, because he does take care of my sons. However, shortly after he raped me, I move out of his house (details to come). I can't live under the same roof with him any longer — the whole situation is unbearable.

However, I still have no money, no green card, no education beyond the 8th grade, and I'm not yet fluent in English. So my job prospects are almost nil.

Further, I'm concerned about leaving Kim behind. As mentioned, she's only 9. I wonder, *Would Rod do something to her?* But Kim's different. Unlike me, she's always had a voice of her own. She has no fear, and she wouldn't hesitate to tell Rod where to get off. (By the time I was 5 I'd already lost my voice in this sense. So saying *no* to father — or later to a stepfather — isn't something I've felt I have the right to do.)

Also, I'm worried that leaving the boys with mother and Rod might harm them emotionally. Because mother abandoned me when I was a child, I've sworn to myself that I'd never abandon my sons. But, this is exactly what I now feel forced to do for the same reason as mother — to escape an abuser.

Narcotics Anonymous and Drew

A month or so before Rod raped me, mother shared with her hairdresser, Elise, about my addiction. Elise happens to be in Alcoholics Anonymous (AA). She suggests that I join a different program, but one that also is based on the "12 Steps": Narcotics Anonymous (NA). (For further information about these programs, see www.aa.org and www.na.org.)

On my behalf, Elise contacts Drew, a very dedicated member of NA who goes out of his way to help newcomers begin their recovery from drug abuse. Drew starts coming every day to Easton to take me to NA meetings in Annapolis. At first, because of my anxiety about Rod (and just general nervousness and insecurity), I have 1 or 2 drinks while waiting for Drew to pick me up. After a week or so, I confide in him that I'm still drinking, because of how I feel still living under the same roof with Rod. Drew explains that I need to get out of that house if I'm ever to get clean and dry.

He offers to let me move in with him at his place in Annapolis. There are 3 other guys living in his house, and all of them are in NA. I decide to make the move. I work for my room and board by doing the cooking and keeping the house clean. In turn, they take me back and forth to NA meetings.

I want to date Drew, because he's now my hero. He has saved me from the untenable situation with Rod. But, Drew deflects my overtures. He explains that he doesn't get romantically involved with newcomers (in keeping with the "suggestions", as they're called, of AA and NA).

Drew regularly goes to NA conventions. In the summer of '83, the East Coast NA Convention is held in Bethlehem, Pennsylvania. Drew invites me to go with him. (I have less than 1 month clean at that point, and even less time sober.) At the convention I meet James, who is in recovery from heroin addiction, which he acquired while serving in Vietnam.

Originally from Brooklyn, James is tall, a little chubby, and 6 years older than I am. He's also kind and caring. Most importantly, I feel protected when I'm with him. After the convention, he goes back to his home in Queens, New York, and I go back to Annapolis. Soon we're dating — he visits me in Annapolis, and I visit him in Queens.

I live at Drew's for about 6 months. But eventually he nudges me into moving out, saying, "You can't cook and clean for us forever. You need a real job to get back on your feet."

Pizza and Calzone: Too Hot to Handle

I still don't have a green card or a work visa. But it's 1983 (long before 9/11), so employers aren't so strict about checking worker ID's. Besides, I do have a valid Social Security number. (Mother got it for me the 1st time I was in America. Back then, even a 15-year-old merely visiting the US could easily get a Social Security card.)

I go to a nearby shopping mall with my Social Security card, and soon have a job at a small pizzeria. I'm working behind the counter, putting pizzas and calzones into an oven, and taking them out when they're done. As a result, I frequently burn myself. (I still have some of the scars.)

I move into an apartment with 2 other girls who are in NA. This is my 1st step toward true independence: making $70 to $80 per week, and living in a $50 a week room.

As my mind clears up from years of drug abuse, the realization comes into sharper focus that because of my addiction, I've forfeited what would have been financial freedom for the rest of my life. In spite of everything father did that was wrong, he worked very hard to make sure I wouldn't have to endure things like being scarred by a pizza oven while working for peanuts. Because of my irresponsible behavior, all that he worked so hard for is gone forever.

And worst of all, I've lost custody of my sons. My goal now is to get my sons back, and to make enough money for the 3 of us to live on our own. But, I have no idea how I'm going to accomplish this. As a relatively recent immigrant making so little, the path to this goal looks long and difficult. I have no savings, no high school diploma, and no sense of self-worth. I feel completely broken.

Italian Fashions

When the Italian clothier Seriano opens a store in the same mall as the pizzeria, I apply for a job there. Although I don't have prior experience in retail sales, they hire me anyway, because I speak Italian fluently.

Retail's tough. I'm on my feet all day, and have to work weekends and holidays. My weekly take-home varies from $150 to $180. It's double my pay making calzones and pizzas, but it's still not very much for a single mother of 2 young boys. The worst part is that my work schedule hardly leaves time to visit my sons, who are still living with mother and Rod.

Soon I'm promoted to manager of the Annapolis store. Next, I help Seriano open a new store in Washington, DC. In the summer of 1984, Seriano asks me to relocate either to Newport Beach, California or to Paramus, New Jersey to train a new owner of a Seriano store at one or the other location. It's no contest — I move in with James in Queens, and begin to help set up the new store in Paramus, a 30-minute commute from James's place.

After I've been at the job in Paramus for a couple of months, Seriano wants to send me to Tysons Corner, a huge shopping mall near Reston, Virginia. They also want me to then help open other stores nationwide. Seriano is paying me more for these assignments — maybe $350 or $400 a week (still not that much, even back then). But they expect me to constantly travel to new-store locations all over America. How would I be able to raise my sons?

𝕸𝖆𝖗𝖗𝖎𝖆𝖌𝖊

At various times in 1983 and 1984, and as late as 1985, I ask mother to help me get a green card. She always responds, "The papers have been filed" — but nothing ever happens. It turns out that mother hasn't done anything about it.

Then in 1985, James proposes to me: "I care about you, and I'd like to help you get your papers. If we marry, you could get a green card, and your mother would probably return custody of your sons."

I ask mother, "Do you think it's a good idea to marry James?" Though she has met him just once, she answers, "Don't worry about it. Marry him. If the marriage doesn't work out, you can always divorce him." (This is the total of mother's advice to me about marriage.)

In February 1985, James and I wed in Baltimore. On the same day, we drive to Easton, where mother returns custody of Johan to me, almost exactly 2 years after she took my boys away from me. We decide that Lukas should continue to live in Easton until he finishes 1st grade. In June 1985, Lukas too comes to live with us. I'm finally reunited with both of my sons.

Before long, I'm working in a Seriano store on Madison Avenue in Manhattan, as a regular sales assistant again. I've accepted this demotion because, as noted, I can't raise my sons properly if I have to move to a new city every 2 or 3 months.

I'm back to earning the minimum wage, which at the time is about $4.50 an hour. And unlike before, I have to pay for a babysitter. It's bad enough that Lukas and Johan weren't with me for much of the 2 years mother had custody of them. Now, *no one* in our family is with them in the daytime. I feel constant guilt, because my sons need my time and attention. And, of course, my feelings about mother abandoning me, and my being raised by father, are far from resolved. This adds greatly to my ongoing emotional turmoil.

Although I'm still fluent in German myself, I don't have time to teach my sons German (or anything else), because I'm in a retail job from 9 AM to 6 PM. I have 20 minutes of lunchtime, spent standing up in the stockroom. Since I have hardly any money after paying rent and feeding my sons, my lunch every day is a 75¢ potato knish with mustard, which I buy from a pushcart on Madison Avenue.

For several years Rod sends me $100 each month, probably out of guilt. Though he never mentions his reason for helping me financially, he knows what he did to me was wrong.

Rage on the Rise

I'm not really in love with James. (After what's happened with Fabio, I'm not even sure what "love" means.) But James is a good guy, so it's sad for both of us that, with the passage of time, I become increasingly distressed by his attempts at physical intimacy — even if he merely tries to hug me or hold my hand. Eventually, I fly into a rage whenever he tries to touch me in a romantic way.

When I was a child, every time I tried to get my hand out from father's grasp, he gripped my hand even tighter. This made me feel rage. So now that I'm an adult, I cannot tolerate handholding at all. For the 1st time in my life, I can exercise enough control over my own body to pull my hand away. And, I'm not calm and composed when I take my hand from James — I *angrily* yank it away from him.

Sometimes James would put his hand on my thigh while we're in the car. This too is a trigger, because it's another thing father used to do — as if I were his girlfriend. I didn't have the right to say, *Don't do that!* If I tried to move my leg away, he'd become furious and grasp my thigh even tighter, with a scary look on his face.

I had to endure father's inappropriately touching me, with my whole being rebelling against it. And during the time I lived with mother and Rod, it would've been too incendiary to express my feelings about Rod's nightly sexual harassment.

Now I have the freedom to say *no.* So when James puts his hand on my leg while he's driving, I sometimes become so enraged that I open the car door, wanting to jump out. I can't be emotionally present for him because I'm too psychologically damaged. Sex with him becomes torture for me. We start having arguments so severe I want to beat him with my fists. I'd get so angry I'd end up sleeping on the floor.

James is the first one to tell me I'm suffering from long-term emotional damage from father's sexual abuse, and I need to seek help. He urges me, "You have incredible intimacy issues. You must go into therapy to get this sorted out."

Moving On

**One day you finally knew what you had to do, and began
... to save the only life you could save.** (Mary Oliver)

Following James's advice, I start therapy. I'm grateful to him for getting me to do this while I'm relatively young: age 26 (as noted, I continue to age 40). But, I still have to leave him. My anger is too great from years of childhood abuse.

One summer weekend in 1985, James goes to the East Coast Narcotics Anonymous Convention — the same convention where we'd met 2 years earlier. But, this time I don't go with him. Instead, I pack my few belongings, take my sons (I've just gotten Lukas back), and move out. (James already knows I've been planning on leaving. He's told me he'd prefer not to be present when I make the move.)

He may have been hoping I wouldn't go through with it, because he knows I have no money and no furniture — actually *no anything*. Nevertheless, I find a 2-bedroom apartment that's only 3 blocks away. (I don't recall for sure, but I think Rod helps me with the deposit and 1ˢᵗ month's rent.)

When I leave James's apartment, I take 3 forks, 3 spoons, 3 dinner knives, 3 plates, a pot, and an iron for pressing clothing. There's a small mattress on the floor that I also take, along with some pillows and a couple of sheets. James has one of those 5-gallon water bottles that he saves quarters in. I take about $50 in quarters, and I leave a note saying I'll return these things once I'm established and can buy my own stuff.

Lukas has just turned 7, and Johan is almost 3½. Walking the 3 blocks from one apartment to the other, we carry in our arms these few items, plus 1 or 2 towels and our clothes.

So this is how my 1ˢᵗ marriage ends. I leave James because he wants an intimacy I can't give to him — or to anyone else.

Fortunately, I do get a green card. I check James's mailbox every day before he gets home, because I fear he will withhold the green card from me as retaliation for my leaving him. In fact, I feel I *deserve* to be punished by him, because that's how it's been my whole life: punishment for expressing my needs or wants. (Looking back, however, I realize that James was much too nice to have done something like that.)

Going It Alone

Now that we're on our own, life is much harder. Luckily, our new apartment's previous occupants left behind a couple of mattresses. (For a long time, we don't even have proper beds.) I use plastic milk crates as dressers. I'm barely making enough money to pay for rent and a babysitter. There isn't enough left over for a healthy diet. For the next several years, my sons and I are poor. Dirt poor.

Cousin Heike, one of uncle Hubert and aunt Maria's daughters, occasionally sends me $100 from Bolzitano. This helps a lot. I might receive $100 in September for my birthday, which would make that month easier, and another $100 for Christmas. And, Rod continues to send $100 here and there. Sophie, a neighborhood woman who is escaping an abusive relationship, rents one of the 2 bedrooms. Lukas and Johan share the other. I sleep on the couch.

What I earn working for Seriano is so little that, even with the help I'm getting, I'm late paying the rent every month — because I buy food instead. Even so, during this period we almost never eat meat, not even chicken. We eat whatever is cheapest: eggs, pasta, vegetable soups, rice with vegetables, rice with beans, bread with butter or jelly. But, almost never meat or fish.

I remember the 1st Christmas on our own, when money from Heike allows me to buy some cold cuts, including salami. Johan, who is then 4 years old and has never eaten salami before, gets so excited that he can't stop telling the neighbors that he has eaten some salami!

The whole situation is emotionally devastating for me. I grew up never wanting for material things. Often there was no food in our house because there was no mother to shop and cook and run the household. But, I still *could* go shopping whenever I wanted to — and father would always pay the bill.

Now I'm in America working full-time, and I don't even have the money to properly feed my sons. What makes me feel even worse is that I know about nutrition. I was aware of the importance of good nutrition when I was growing up. I know the difference between food that's healthy and food that isn't (one of father's good influences).

When Lukas was born, I tried everything to keep him healthy. I breastfed him and cooked fresh vegetables for him. Every meal was homemade. He didn't have any sugar until he was 3. Even his store-bought baby food was organic (which was already available in the Berlin of 1978-1979).

I didn't have much money while raising Lukas in Germany either. As noted, I was on welfare. But, I worked (off the books) part time as a maid in the landlord's bread-and-breakfast. Plus, Fabio was the babysitter. Combined with welfare, I had enough money to buy organic spinach and carrots, as well as other organic foods for Lukas.

So, I *know* what my sons need nutritionally. That I now can't afford to buy healthy food for them is heartbreaking. And, there would have been plenty of money for feeding my sons, and for much else, if I hadn't squandered my inheritance on drugs and drug-addled bad choices. This awareness greatly increases the guilt I'm feeling.

Instead of eating healthy foods in their early years living under my roof, my sons eat lots of starch and refined carbohydrates — like pizza from Raffaele's Pizzeria in Astoria. Raffaele is a good friend. He often gives us free pizza, because he knows we're poor. It may not seem like much, but for us it's a very big gift. Still, my boys should be eating a more balanced diet.

Now that I'm the head of the household, we're barely getting by. I constantly feel overwhelmed and anxious. At Seriano I'm taking home a little over $1,000 a month. The rent on our apartment is $600, and the babysitter is $400 or $500, depending. So there's hardly enough money for food, much less for clothing and other necessities. And we don't have health insurance.

Even with the periodic $100 from Rod or Heike, I'm not making it. Although I've been off heroin for 3 years, and am working 6 days a week, I'm still unable to give my sons the care they need and deserve. We just survive from one day to the next.

Mad Men (and Women)

Walking along Madison Avenue, I pass Orietta, another up-market Italian clothier. A sign in their window indicates they are seeking an experienced salesperson. I go in and apply. They hire me on the spot, because I speak Italian fluently and I have solid experience with Seriano.

Orietta doesn't pay more base salary, but they do pay a commission on sales, so it's an opportunity to make a bit more money. At Orietta, I'm making about $300 a week, totaling almost $1,300 a month. I can buy better food for my sons and myself — and still pay the rent and phone bill on time.

We soon move into an apartment that's a little better. (Sophie comes with us.) It costs $700 per month, and a babysitter continues to cost $400 or $500. So, we still wind up with nothing at month's end.

After Orietta, I go to work for yet another clothing retailer, Bottega Milano. In the next few years, I work at a number of other jobs. But, I still can't find one that pays enough money to decently support myself and my sons.

Babysitters

The situation with babysitters is completely nerve wracking. I'm really frightened, not knowing whom to trust with watching my sons. The babysitters come in every hue — so their color is not the issue. Instead, it's things like the one who, when I get home, is lounging on my couch eating chips and slurping beer — ignoring my sons. Another babysitter has the kids watching a gruesome horror movie — when Johan is only 4 years old. A different babysitter allows Lukas to sit on the hood of her car while it's in motion! Then there's the woman who falls on my carpet while she's horsing around with Johan. And, there's the one who ups and leaves some time earlier in the day, so my sons are alone until I get home that evening.

I have no family support to speak of. Mother rarely visits; at the time, we don't even talk much. As a single mom of 2 small sons, I'm living a nightmare.

The Old Buick

I'm constantly trying to find a way to lift my little family out of poverty. In 1986, I pass the exam to become a real estate agent, so I can sell homes in and about my neighborhood in Queens. I'll be working closer to home, so I won't be away from Johan and Lukas 11 or 12 hours a day, 6 days a week. And, I hope to finally be able to make ends meet financially.

But, to sell real estate in suburban Queens, I must have a car to take clients from house to house. I've recently come by about $800. (It may have been from a tax refund.) Whatever the source, it's a lot of money at this time in my life.

I use it to buy a car owned by a family in Queens. Although it comes recommended by someone I know, the car turns out to be a lemon — it runs for just 3 days, and then breaks down. I'm devastated. I've been thinking that my sons and I are moving up the ladder. I call the family I bought the car from and tell them it's no longer running. They say that's too bad — *I* bought it, so *I* have to deal with it.

Shortly afterward, I meet Trent, while I'm traveling with the boys on a train from Washington, DC back to Queens, having just visited mother. Trent is also returning to New York, after visiting his girlfriend in Alexandria, Virginia.

In the course of our conversation, I mention my car dilemma. He responds, "Here's what we can do: I have 3 cars, and I've been letting my 17-year-old daughter use 1 of them. She lives with my ex-wife, Cara, in Virginia Beach. My daughter got into a fender-bender because she was drinking and driving. My ex-wife no longer allows her to drive the car, because Cara now realizes our daughter is too immature. The car is currently sitting in their driveway, just taking up space. I'll call and tell Cara you'll come and pick it up. I don't want any money. Just come and take it."

When I get back to New York, I call Cara myself. Trent has already spoken to her. She tells me, "This is great. The car will no longer be a burden to us — and it's running fine. You can come pick it up when you're ready."

Risky Business

When you got nothing, you got nothing to lose. (Bob Dylan)

Because I've lost almost everything, I'm more willing to take risks. If my life were less precarious, I certainly wouldn't have traveled with my 2 sons to Virginia Beach, Virginia to pick up an auto from a stranger's ex-wife.

Mother helps pay for the 3 of us to fly to Virginia Beach (for which I'm still grateful). Cara and her new husband pick us up at the airport. They seem like nice people.

The car is a big boxy turquoise-blue Buick from the 1970's — sort of a cabin cruiser on wheels. A large mat covers the rusted out hole in the floor, blocking sight of the pavement below. Yet they assure me the car runs okay, and should make it to New York without trouble. However, they point out, it needs inspection, registration, and insurance.

But I hardly have any money — maybe $30. It's enough for gas and perhaps a meal for the 3 of us along the way. I think to myself, *I don't have the time or the money for all of us to stay here while I go to the DMV to register the car, plus buy auto insurance. What the heck — I'm just going to leave!*

The whole thing is nuts: I'm with my 2 young sons driving this huge old Buick with no license plates back to New York, hoping and praying the police don't stop us. But this is the kind of thing people do when they don't have other options.

While we're on the highway driving north through rural Virginia, the engine suddenly conks out. There's no sound coming from under the hood, and the car feels like a glider gradually slowing and losing altitude.

In spite of the power steering and power brakes no longer working, I manage to pull over onto the auxiliary lane. At the time, I'm 28, or close to it. Lukas is 8, and Johan is 4. I'm wondering, *What are we going to do? I can't call the police, because I'm totally illegal driving this car!*

Answered Prayers

I decide to take all our belongings, leave the car, and just keep walking until we find help. (I have no idea what else to do.) The 3 of us begin trooping along the side of the highway. I'm silently praying, *God, we really need Your help now. I'm scared, and I have no idea what's going to happen to us.*

After walking for some time, my sons are getting increasingly tired and anxious. They start asking questions like: "What's going on? Where are we going? Who's going to help us?" I tell them, "We have no choice. We have to do this. We have to keep walking."

At last, we see a ranch house set back a good distance from the highway, as is often the case out in the country. I say to the boys, "Look, there's a home — maybe they'll help us."

We walk down the long driveway until we reach the house. I knock on the front door. A woman opens the door, and I start to explain why we're there. In order to put us at ease, she gently interrupts, "Oh, don't worry, you just come right in. We've had people here before whose car has broken down on the highway. When they come to our door, we invite them in."

Surprised, I reply, "Really?" She responds, "Of course. Come in. We'll get you a tow truck and whatever else you need."

We enter the charming home of Sue and Jeff. They're probably in their early 30's, with 2 children, a couple of cats, 2 dogs, and a pond filled with fish in their backyard.

To further put us at ease, Sue adds, "You must be hungry. Sit down and relax." While she's preparing something for us to eat, her kids and mine are playing with a puppy and the cats. It's like paradise. Jeff and Sue turn out to be the most lovely people imaginable. I start crying, because I'm so moved by their kindness.

Jeff handles the whole thing. He knows a local tow truck operator and a nearby auto repair garage. After making arrangements over the phone, he goes to my car, by himself, to meet the tow truck driver.

It's late afternoon when the garage calls. After he gets off the phone, Jeff says, "They've checked out your car. The timing belt broke. They don't have a replacement in stock, and it's too late to get one today. But, they've put in an order. It'll arrive tomorrow and be installed then."

They invite us to join them for dinner and spend the night at their home. I think to myself, *So this is what the rural South is like.*

The next day I call mother. She agrees to pay for the car repair with her credit card — if it's okay with the repair shop. This is quite nice of her. She doesn't usually help me with money, but she does for this trip.

Jeff takes me to the auto repair shop. I explain my situation to the mechanic, who says, "No problem. Have your mother call us with her credit card number. The car should be ready this afternoon."

The boys and I leave later that day. I can't believe we have met such nice people. My prayers from the previous morning, while the 3 of us were walking along the highway, have been amply answered.

We head to Maryland, because mother wants us to visit her on our way back. The car is running fine, but it's still illegal for me to be driving it without a registration or even license plates, much less insurance. I'm also worried that something else will go wrong with the car. We may not be so lucky if we get stuck on the highway a 2nd time.

We arrive at mother's house without further incident. Rod is there(!) By this time mother and Rod are separated, but amicably so. (I don't know why he's there, but mother must have told him I'm coming.)

Mother has often seemed oddly detached from things going on right before her eyes — if she prefers not to see them. I've already written about the nude photographs of Margit and me when we were children, which father sent to mother — without her demurring at all, as far as I am aware. I've also mentioned the time we were in the kitchen, having a typical mother-daughter conversation, when a syringe and spoon fell out of my boot as mother was helping me remove it — and she pretended not to notice. And, I've mentioned her enthusiasm, in spite of my heroin-induced nodding, during my spending spree for custom furnishings and expensive cars.

Though not as extreme as those examples, there's a similarity in mother's nonchalance about my driving to New York —

with her 2 grandsons — in a rusty old car that has no license plates, no registration, no up-to-date inspection sticker, and no insurance. Mother and Rod both seem to be totally okay with me driving this car up the East Coast!

To this day, it seems strange to me. If this were one of my sons, I'd tell him, "You're not going to drive this car yet. I'll help you, but you're going to stay here until the car is registered, and has license plates and insurance. Otherwise, it's not legal — what if something happens?" But mother and Rod merely wish us good luck, and wave goodbye as we drive off. Fortunately, this time we get all the way to New York without further incident.

It seems crazy when I think about it today, that I would take this risk — especially after already breaking down on the road once. But I take such risks because I feel I have no realistic alternative.

Auto (un)Insurance

Once back in New York, I start work as a real estate agent. As intended, I use the Buick to show clients homes in suburban Queens. The car works fine for taking my sons back and forth to school as well. And, now I can spend more time at home with them.

I soon register the car, put on plates, and get it inspected. But, I don't have nearly enough money to insure it, which would cost at least $1,500. However, there are people in the neighborhood who for $250 will sell a fake insurance card that claims to be valid for a year. I understand that a lot of immigrants do this — and now I'm one of them.

There are other illegal things going on in the neighborhood. Petty stuff. For example, it seems that everyone on our block has an illegal cable TV hookup. Everyone except us. I remember one of my sons asking, "Mom, why are you paying for cable? No one else is."

I explain to him that I pay for cable because I think it's the right thing to do. I will cut corners if I feel it is essential for our well-being; but cable tv is a luxury, not a necessity.

By contrast, I don't see driving my rusty old Buick as a luxury. I see it as required for supporting myself and my sons.

Since I can't afford a real policy, I buy a fake insurance card. If the police stop me for a driving infraction, I can show them the card. But, as shall be seen, if I'm in a serious accident, I'll have a big problem.

This is another example of the risks I take because I have so few options. I'm scared initially, but after a time I don't even think about it. I drive this old Buick without insurance for the 2 years that I'm working in suburban real estate — basically until the car is no longer worth repairing.

𝔐𝔞𝔫𝔥𝔞𝔱𝔱𝔞𝔫 𝔗𝔯𝔞𝔫𝔰𝔣𝔢𝔯

Working strictly on commission is a tough way to raise a family. Some months I make enough money; other months I do not. If I don't sell enough, we don't eat.

I'm young and inexperienced at real estate sales and rentals. And, I don't deal well with rejection. So I'm not a great agent, merely an okay one. Also, I get tired of using my time and energy to drive people around for weeks, and right when I think they're finally ready to buy a property, all of a sudden they tell me something like their aunt died in Connecticut leaving them her house, so they're moving there, instead of staying in Queens. I'd feel, *Oh that's great — all my effort was completely wasted!*

Because I'm still not earning enough to pay my bills, in 1988 I give up house sales in Queens. Harriet, a neighbor of mine, tells me about Roni, a real estate broker in Manhattan. His company handles Manhattan rentals only. She adds, "He's pretty busy, so you might do well there."

I'm not eager to go back to working in Manhattan, because the time spent commuting there and back is time I'm not with Lukas and Johan. Plus, there's the issue of finding a babysitter who'll work the longer hours resulting from my extra travel time. But, I decide to give it a try anyway. Since I now have experience in real estate, Roni hires me.

Unfortunately, Roni requires all of us to work for him 6 days a week. This, despite the fact that the reason real estate brokers can avoid paying their agents a base salary (and instead have them work strictly on commission) is that agents are legally "independent contractors" — and thus (supposedly) free to negotiate their own terms of employment, including work schedules. In other words, because technically we're free agents rather than Roni's employees, he can't legally dictate that we work 6 days a week. (His trying to have it both ways eventually gets him into big trouble.)

While working for Roni, I help Vinnie, a mob-connected guy in his 50's, find an apartment for a son of his. For awhile afterward, Vinnie is an emotional caretaker for me, and sometimes helps me financially. After the Buick dies, he co-signs the loan I take out to purchase a new Hyundai hatchback (one of the least expensive cars on the market at the time).

Now I'm merrily driving my sons around Queens in my little hatchback, as well as showing well-off clients luxury apartments located in upmarket Manhattan neighborhoods. Sometimes the doorman allows me to park in the building's garage. But at other times, I have to park on the street. Because I can't take up too much of the client's time, I sometimes park illegally. Since I still make only a little money in some months, I don't always pay the tickets. Even in good months, there are often necessities that come first. Hence, the unpaid parking tickets continue to pile up.

I work for Roni for 2 years. As with selling homes in Queens, this job is also quite stressful, because my monthly income is never consistent. Although it's much easier to get a renter to commit to an apartment with a 1- or 2-year lease than it is to get a buyer to purchase a home with a 20- or 30-year mortgage, there are still some months when I don't make enough money to support myself and my sons. As a mother, this is very hard for me to deal with.

When Lukas is only 12, I have him taking care of himself, as well as watching 8-year-old Johan, from the time the 2 of them get out of school until I get home. I know this is putting too much responsibility on Lukas, and it's another thing I constantly feel guilty about.

After a time, all the stress gets to be too much, and I quit working for Roni. I assume I don't qualify for unemployment benefits, because I chose to leave the job, rather than being fired or laid off. But, friends advise me to apply anyway, and I figure there's little to lose by trying.

A clerk at the unemployment insurance office tells me that I actually might be eligible, so I submit an application. But soon, another clerk informs me that Roni hasn't paid into the unemployment fund (by claiming we are independent contractors), so there's no money out of which to pay me.

I find out later that as a result of my application for benefits, the NY State Labor Department investigates Roni. I run into Harriet, the friend who told me about Roni in the 1st place.

She tells me, "You got Roni into trouble. He had to pay a big fine to the Labor Department." I feel bad about this. Roni hired me when I needed a job, and he wasn't a bad boss. I never meant to get him into trouble, but I was unaware of the workings of New York State's labor laws.

Hit and Run

In the early 1990's, my employer of the time invites me to join her and her adult daughter to see the musical *Phantom of the Opera*, which is then playing on Broadway in Manhattan. While driving home after the show, I stop at a traffic light on Northern Boulevard in Queens. There's a commercial panel truck waiting in front of me. Suddenly, I see in my rearview mirror a car racing up from behind. I think to myself, *Oh my God, it's going to plow right into me* — just as the car does crash into the rear of my little Hyundai!

My head slams into the windshield, and my thumb jams into the steering wheel, popping out of its socket. I look in the mirror and see an egg-sized lump growing out from my forehead. I'm in shock. The car that's rammed me has crushed my hatchback's rear, and pushed me into the van ahead with such violent force that my car's front is flattened too. I try to open the door, but it's stuck because the whole car is now like a collapsed accordion. I'm trapped — and freaking out.

Perhaps it's my karma (for causing the Fiat 500 to flip onto its side on my way to Verona, but not stopping until the return trip), because the guy who has plowed into my Hyundai backs up and speeds off. I'm thinking, *He's driving away, even though I could be dying.* But a cab driver who has seen what happened begins chasing him, and another car joins the chase. They catch up with this hit-and-run driver and hold him until police arrive.

The police take my information, and I show them my phony insurance card. I'm then taken in an ambulance to a nearby hospital for a few hours. While I'm there under observation and awaiting test results, the police come to visit me. They tell me that although the other driver is clearly at fault, he has no insurance — and neither do I.

Now I'm scared. I've been keeping up with the car payments on the Hyundai every month, but I haven't yet had the money to buy insurance (or pay for the mounting stack of parking tickets). Instead, I've continued to buy a phony insurance card every year.

Nowadays, NYC police are strict about arresting drivers who don't have insurance. But back then, they don't treat it as seriously. However, though I'm not in legal trouble, the driver who destroyed my car won't be paying for the damage he's done.

I'm still in shock, my head hurts, and I don't know yet if my thumb is broken. I have a slight concussion and a huge bump on my forehead. But, the hospital lets me leave that night. I don't remember how I got home. (I must have taken a taxi.)

The next day, with a bump on my forehead, my head pounding, and my neck hurting from whiplash, I'm back at work. I can't *not* work, because I need to make money — including still having to make payments on the Hyundai, even though it's a total loss.

Raj, a friend of mine, after hearing of my plight offers me his old Volvo station wagon. It dribbles a little oil from the exhaust, but I don't care. (I drive this Volvo for maybe 2 or 3 years, before it breaks down for the last time.)

When I first get the car, I say to myself, *I now know from losing the Hyundai that I can't use a phony insurance card anymore. I'm going to get my car properly insured — and still try to pay the rest of my bills.*

Run DMV

I go to the Department of Motor Vehicles to register the Volvo, expecting to 1st have to pay my outstanding parking tickets. I say to a clerk working behind the counter, "I'd like to make a payment plan for the parking tickets I haven't yet paid."

But after the clerk runs my information through the DMV computer, she says, "You don't owe for any parking tickets."

However, a letter from the DMV has already notified me that I owe about $4,000(!) in parking tickets, including interest and penalties for late payment. Since I want to register my car (and I don't want the interest and penalties to continue to accumulate), I ask the clerk, "Please check again, because I need to resolve this so I can register my car today."

She checks the computer again, and then says, "You don't owe anything."

I respond, "That's impossible."

She replies (with her voice rising in volume), "Lady, do you *want* to pay for tickets!? You don't owe anything!"

I later learn that when the New York City DMV first computerized their records, there were a lot of mistakes. Some people were charged for parking tickets they hadn't received. Some, like me, who did have unpaid tickets, nevertheless wound up with a clean slate. Perhaps it was nothing more than a simple computer glitch, but to me it felt like divine intervention.

I still have to make payments of $150 a month on a Hyundai that's on some scrap heap. But, I've been blessed with not owing any parking tickets, and at least I now have a Volvo station wagon to get around in.

Amazing Grace

The combination of these events seems to me like more than mere coincidence. I feel that God has definitely looked out for my boys and me.

We have next to nothing when we arrive in America. And, I'm so naive back then! When I knock on the door of strangers in rural Virginia, we could've been held for ransom — or worse. Instead, Sue and Jeff turn out to be a kind and helpful couple, who go out of their way to help us.

For a time, I stay in touch with Trent, the man who gave me the Buick. On one occasion, Trent and his girlfriend invite my sons and me up to Lake George, where they have a winter rental. We have a wonderful weekend there. After a time, Trent and I lose contact. But I'll always remember him as a warm and generous man. He didn't have to give me a car. Even though it was old, he could have sold it and gotten some money for it.

Vinnie didn't have to co-sign the loan on the Hyundai (which I did pay in full). There was nothing in it for him — other than whatever satisfaction he felt from helping out someone in need.

When the Hyundai is totaled, a Volvo is given to me by my friend Raj. So, I'm given 2 cars for free. (Plus, there's all the free pizza from Raffaele!)

These are some of the decent men and women who've been generous in helping me out at different times in my life. I have to say I feel blessed to have known them.

There are other things that happen that I think are through the mercy of a Higher Power. For instance, when the $4,000 I owe in parking tickets vanishes from the DMV's records.

I feel this all has happened through God's Grace, and I would not be alive otherwise.

In other words, *I believe.*

𝕵𝖔𝖊 (𝖓𝖔𝖙 𝖘𝖔) 𝕶𝖊𝖜𝖑

In 1986, while I'm still a sales assistant at Orietta, the jazz great Joe Kewl walks into the store (with his entourage). I'm standing by the counter, sketching on a piece of paper. (In those days, I'm always sketching, drawing, doodling. Perhaps I haven't gotten over not going to art school.) Joe tells another girl who's working there that he wants *me* to help him. I walk over to him (having no idea who he is). He looks at me, and then in his sexy voice says something quite impertinent. I won't quote his exact words, but in essence he congratulates himself on his virile reaction to me.

Looking at what I'm sketching, Joe then says, "I like what you're doing." (My artistry may have been one of the reasons he's attracted to me, as shall be seen.) Along the side of my drawing, he writes his telephone number, and tells me to call him. I then give him *my* phone number, and tell him if he wants to speak with me, *he'll* have to be the one who calls.

I don't give him much thought after he walks out of the store. Lots of men have given me their phone number. (It goes with the territory of being an unattached woman living in New York.) I know hardly anything about American pop culture. I certainly wasn't into celebrities during my "lost years" doing drugs back in Italy. And, by the time I come to America in the early 1980's, the peak of Joe's fame has passed (though he's still an iconic figure in the jazz world).

But, my co-workers at Orietta fill me in that Joe is rich and famous. That same night, he does call me, and we talk for a bit. Because he's 60 at the time, and I'm 27, Joe is kind of a father-figure for me — something I've missed since my real father died 6 years earlier.

Soon, we're dating. Joe comes to Astoria in his limo to visit me, and I visit him in his apartment at the Norfolk on 5th Avenue in Manhattan. My first time at his place, I notice that there are a woman's belongings in his apartment. I ask Joe about it. He explains that his ex-wife, a famous entertainer in her own right, uses his apartment when she's in NYC, since their divorce is amicable.

Advance Warning

A part of me realizes from the get-go that Joe's not someone I should go out with. Early on, I notice he's using black beauties (*ie,* amphetamines). Soon I discover he's using codeine too. In fact, he has a little black bag full of pills.

At my next group therapy session, I mention that I'm dating Joe. By pure coincidence, 4 of the men in the group have been sidemen for him at one time or another. So they know he uses drugs. They warn me that I might relapse if I continue seeing him. And, that I have to be very careful when I'm with him, because he's also abusive.

But, I ignore their warnings, as well as my own better judgment. I learned a long time ago how to deal with a dangerous man, so I figure I'll be okay with Joe.

A Tale of Two Cities

Father used to take me to beautiful resorts, where we'd stay in luxury hotels. In spite of my years as a hippie, there's a part of me that still enjoys this side of life — for example being in Joe's luxurious apartment overlooking Central Park.

Dating him is so different from the poverty I've experienced since leaving James. Joe invites me to join him in New Orleans at a jazz festival he's performing in. We stay at an elegant hotel, and dine in expensive restaurants. Spending time with Joe gives me hope that somehow I'll one day get out of poverty. Not necessarily through him. But even briefly being around people with money boosts my spirit.

I've come to realize how extreme New York's inequality is. There are the very poor — the homeless New Yorkers who have nothing and struggle just to survive from one day to the next. Then there are the working poor, who sit in the subway like they're already dead. Yet they do this every day.

I mentioned earlier that Sophie has been boarding with us, both in our 1st apartment and in our current one. I originally connected with her when she responded to a room-for-rent flyer I'd placed in a local supermarket. She was then living in her car, after leaving an abusive relationship. The required 3 months' rent to move into an NYC apartment (especially since rents are so high) was more than she could get together at one time — even though she was holding down a regular job.

And then, there are the lucky few — like Joe. He lives in a ritzy hotel alongside Central Park, and is driven here and there in a limousine. Joe gives me the phone number of his chauffeur, Candace. Anytime I need a ride, I can call her and say, "Candace, please pick me up at (wherever)", and she'd give me a lift home. It's kind of a shock (a pleasant one) to go from no food in the house to being driven home in a limo.

Not that Joe is very generous. He does have generous moments now and then, but they're rare.

Art House

When he's in New York, Joe might phone and say, "*Fraulein*, I'm coming over tonight." But, he's not the type to merely sit still and relax. Joe is always full of energy and creativity. While he visits, he works on a bunch of sketches, at which he's quite talented. Since he likes the way I work with colors, he provides me with tools to color them in. My detail work takes longer than his sketching, so he often leaves the pieces behind for me to finish later.

Abuse

By 1987, although I'm still seeing Joe, our relationship has gone downhill. On one of his European tours, we spend a day in Rome; then on to Torino, Italy; next to Montreux, Switzerland; and after that to Hamburg, Germany — staying in a glamorous hotel at each destination.

While we're in Torino, we get into a big fight. Because he's so fundamentally insecure, Joe doesn't want me to speak Italian to the limo driver. He says to me, in a threatening tone, "Don't *ever* speak Italian in front of me again." But when we get to the hotel, he wants me to tell the concierge that he's not happy with the room, and he wants a different one. I say to him, "You don't want me to speak Italian — so you do it."

He slaps my face. I slap him back, and say, "You know what, Joe? I can walk out of here. Don't forget: This is my home country. I'm quite familiar with my surroundings. I don't really need you."

He soon brings me a plate of food and says, "I'm sorry."

When we get to Hamburg, there's more conflict. He's jealous because I'm talking with one of his stage managers, this time in German. We fight. We make up. We're on-and-off and then back on — a love-hate kind of thing.

Later, I'm back home in Astoria. Joe calls me from Israel — at 4 AM New York time. He shouts over the phone, "Bitch, who did you f*** last night?" I start crying. Then he apologizes and says, "I want you to listen to my sax, fraulein."

Push-Ups

Sometime later, all 4 of my wisdom teeth get pulled in a single dental appointment. Because I'm in a great deal of pain, the dentist gives me a prescription for a narcotic pain reliever. However, since I've been drug-free for about 3 years, I don't have the prescription filled.

But, while I'm serving customers at Bottega Milano, I'm crying because I'm in so much pain. The manager asks, "What's the matter?" I tell her that I've just had oral surgery, but I'm in recovery from drug addiction, so I'm afraid to take the painkiller prescribed by the dentist.

She responds, "If you've been given a prescription for the pain, go fill it. You can't be in this much pain and still work."

So, my manager has given me a green light to fill a prescription for acetaminophen plus codeine. There's a saying in AA and NA: *While you're clean and dry, your disease is doing push-ups.* In other words, if you pick up alcohol or other drugs after a long period of abstinence, it's not as if the clock has been been reset to zero. On the contrary, it's like your addiction has been getting steadily worse the whole time. But you don't know it unless you relapse. Then you find out with a bang. I remember taking just 1 capsule, and suddenly feeling like I've shot heroin. (But, likewise, the pain is gone.)

It's a stressful time with my boys. They're good kids, but they're quite active, and there's no father-figure in the home. Johan, in particular, has no fear — he's a daredevil (like father). I have to constantly watch him. Working full time while raising 2 boys by myself is seriously challenging. Codeine takes the edge off the stress. I'm calmer with my sons (and

I'm better able to endure Joe).

I no longer see him that often. Mostly we talk on the phone. It's flattering to be called by one of the greats of jazz from different cities all over the world, and listen to him play his sax just for me. Then again, as noted, he might say something mean, and I'd cry.

By this time, I've been in therapy long enough to know that I don't deserve to be verbally abused. But, it's still difficult to extract myself from the relationship.

Joe's Gallant Suggestion

Joe is pretty stingy with money — considering how much he has. At the time some people think, *Ah, she has a wealthy man taking care of her.* But, this isn't the case. He gives me $100 here and there, but only rarely.

To his credit, Joe helps me with my dental bills — at first. However, one day when I go to my dentist for an appointment, he says, "I'm sorry, Joe is no longer covering your bill. Unless I'm paid by you, I can't see you anymore."

Regarding my financial straits, at some point Joe suggests I ought to become a call girl. (I think it's his chauvinistic idea of a compliment.) I've always thought that I'm not pretty enough to be a call girl. And, I've never liked my body. I assume that call girls have to be absolutely stunning — and have large breasts, like Pamela Anderson or Dolly Parton.

So, in addition to the obvious "ick" factor, I don't believe I'm attractive enough to succeed as an escort.

Art is Long

As mentioned, whenever Joe comes to my house, he brings a sketchbook and felt-tip markers, charcoals, or pastels. He'd usually draw female figures; then I'd color them in, doing very detailed work. I can't keep up with him, since we have different styles. When I paint, it can take me a few weeks to finish one piece. Joe might do a few sketches in a night.

Page 175: Joe also suggests I try fashion modeling, and pays for test shots. But, due to lack of confidence, I don't pursue it.

After awhile, a suitcase under my bed fills up with his drawings and sketches, in various stages of completion. Some of them are finished pieces, already colored in by me. Some are still basic sketches. Only 30 or 40 are signed by Joe, but anyone who is familiar with Joe's work can tell that the unsigned ones are also by him. There are about 150 in all, but at the time I don't give them a 2nd thought. (What becomes of these sketches is revealed in Book II.)

The End of the Affair

Joe and I date for about 2 years. Going out with him is obviously exciting. I'm already familiar with madmen who have lots of money (because father and his posse of crazy ex-Nazis seemed to always have lots of cash). Perhaps because Joe radiates a similar devil-may-care glamour, I'm attracted to him at first. But behind the so-called glamour, Joe is cheap, abusive, and mean.

Eventually, things come to a head. I have a key to Joe's suite. No one interferes with my coming and going, since everyone who works at the Norfolk knows me. One day I go up to Joe's place, and another woman is there (and she isn't his ex-wife). I slap Joe in the face. He hits me back. Then I pick up a chair and throw it at him, shouting that it's over — I'm not going to be in his life anymore. This is how it ends.

By now it's 1988. I haven't been going to NA meetings, and I've been using more codeine than I was right after my dental surgery. In the past, when Joe was going to be staying overnight or the weekend, at his behest I'd ask his Manhattan doctor to call in a drug prescription to a pharmacy near me in Astoria. I'd then be the one who picks up the order.

After I break up with Joe, I continue calling his doctor and telling him Joe is staying at my house. He'd then call my local drug store and prescribe 100 acetaminophens with codeine. I get away with this for awhile. But, one day his doctor says to me that Joe called for a prescription the day before. He then asks, "Why would Joe call again so soon?" I get scared and never call again.

This ends my free supply of narcotics. I didn't really overdo it. I was taking just 1 or 1½ capsules per day. I knew that with my history I had to be careful. I do think it helped me, because I was so anxious during this period — never having enough money, and yet not having enough time to care for Johan and Lukas either.

Life is Brief — Art is Long.

In a couple of years, Joe becomes gravely ill. Feeling sorry for him, I visit Joe at New York Hospital. By then, diabetes has severely damaged a number of his organs. He's been abusing his health for some time. For example, in spite of having diabetes, he'd eat a pint of Häagen-Dazs ice cream almost every night. (Butterscotch was his favorite flavor.)

Joe dies in 1991, at age 65. But he will always be one of the best known jazz icons.

Carlos

One of my friends in real estate is also a part-time bartender at Riverrun, a well known bar in the Chelsea district of Manhattan. She and another friend from work keep telling me it's a lot of fun, and often invite me to join them there. I go a few times. However, I'm not much of a bar person.

But one evening while at Riverrun, I meet Carlos, a handsome guy who works as an engineer for a large local utility, with a strong union, good pay, and solid benefits. When we meet, I'm unaware that he has a serious cocaine problem. He's not talkative, much less grandiose, like typical coke addicts. Instead, he's calm and gentlemanly, even self-effacing. After my experience with the egomaniacal Joe, a man somewhat like father, I gravitate back to a man who's more like Fabio — except that, unlike Fabio, Carlos has a steady job.

We start dating, and it isn't long before I notice that Carlos always has with him one of those little amber-colored cocaine bottles with a tiny spoon hanging from the underside of its black plastic cap. I've never been into cocaine, but I use a little with him. It does give me energy but, by the same token, it keeps me up at night.

Moving Up

Soon, Carlos is living with us in Astoria. He treats my sons well, and helps a lot financially, for example with the rent and the payments on the Hyundai. (This is before the wreck.)

Carlos has a son from a previous marriage, Paris, whom Carlos has not been visiting because he's not on good terms with Paris's mother. Due to my own abandonment issues, I encourage Carlos to start seeing Paris again. Soon we are getting together with Paris regularly on weekends. He becomes part of our life. For example, the 5 of us go on a vacation to Disney World.

It feels like my sons and I have moved up a little bit. We're no longer poor, because Carlos provides steady support. He's always kind, never abusive. My sons get along well with him. After a struggle, he gets off cocaine and wants to marry me.

He'd likely be a good husband. But, as with James, after awhile I can't tolerate being physically close with Carlos. Paradoxically, I miss him when he's at work. Yet as soon as he gets home, I can't stand his wanting to get close. I really suffer when he tries to touch me, and yet I feel terribly guilty about pushing him away, because he's being very good to me.

I'm still so damaged by father's physical, verbal, and sexual abuse that even if a man treats me well, I can't be intimate with him. So, I sabotage my relationship with Carlos by keeping him at a distance.

Freak Out

Early on, I do a bit of cocaine with him on weekends. But I soon realize that it makes me paranoid. Plus, whenever I use it, I get hooked for that night, and keep wanting more. This increasingly worries me.

Then one morning while I'm in the shower, I start to freak out. My heart is beating out of my chest, and I'm suddenly terrified of letting the water touch my skin. I think to myself, *Oh my God, I have to do another line of coke just to calm down — what am I doing to myself?!* I realize cocaine is going to kill me if I don't stop using it. I'd rather do heroin or another narcotic any day. So, my cocaine use doesn't last long.

By the same token, I'm beginning to lose respect for Carlos, because his cocaine abuse keeps getting worse. Eventually, he seems to be using it all the time.

Strike!

In the summer of 1989, Carlos's union goes out on strike. He doesn't get his regular paycheck from his employer for the 4 months the strike lasts. But, this doesn't reduce his cocaine consumption. If anything it increases, because he now has more time on his hands. Consequently, I've reverted to not being able to pay the rent on time.

When the strike ends in November and he returns to work, his cocaine abuse finally catches up with him. He's arrived late too many times because, for example, he's been up all night doing crossword puzzles. (I'd then have to drive him to work in a hurry.)

The human resources department at his job tells him he has to get treatment. He's sent to a fancy rehab in Florida, which his job-based health insurance is paying for.

Fear of Homelessness

I'm on my own again, without any financial help to speak of. Christmas is coming in a few weeks, and since Carlos didn't get paid while in rehab, I'm 3 months behind in my rent.

I go to the New York City welfare department to get help with food and rent. They tell me the best they can do is to put me and my sons into a shelter for the homeless. The thought of going into a homeless shelter as a single woman with 2 young children (especially in the New York City of 1989) is really frightening to me.

Carlos returns from rehab in early 1990, and starts going to AA and NA meetings. He gets a "sponsor" (ie, someone with long-term abstinence who helps a newcomer), works the 12 Steps, and stays clean and sober. But at this point, I want Carlos out of my life in the worst way.

Still, I don't want to hurt Carlos, because he's always treated me well. He doesn't deserve to be hurt. So, at first I just tell him I'm really happy that he's recovering.

But though we stay together a little while longer, I can't go on living with him. I desperately want out. Since I don't want him to relapse on drugs and alcohol, I try to be gentle when I tell him I need to be free. He's heartbroken at this turn of events, but fortunately he doesn't go back to using cocaine.

In February 1990, Carlos moves into his own apartment. He still tries to mend the relationship. But I felt like a caged animal when we lived together. I feel so much better, and so much freer, living on my own again.

There's no going back now.

Noli Me Tengere
(Don't touch me)

When I was still using heroin, I was tamping down the anger that was bubbling below the surface. However, once I get clean and dry, my emotions emerge at their full strength, especially my rage. I've felt a certain amount of anger since I was a child, but I had no idea just how much fury I've had inside of me all this time.

Carlos continues to want to marry me. He's a good man, but I can't endure him anymore. It's not just Carlos; it now happens with *every* man I date. I become furious if any man wants to get physically or even emotionally close to me. I have moments when I want to strangle whichever man I'm with at the time.

Now that I'm free, I don't want to go back to depending on a man for support. I say to myself, *There's so much money in this city that there's got to be a better way. I can't live with a man, but my sons and I can't continue living in poverty either — it's just too hard.*

𝕍iva 𝔇evorah
Agora Training

Back in 1988 — soon after I break up with Joe, but before I start dating Carlos — I meet Najar in the course of my real estate work. Najar is in his late 30's and quite handsome. Besides buying and selling residential and commercial properties, he also has a carpet store on Broadway in the West 20's, along with a nearby apartment he stays in.

We start dating. It isn't anything serious, but he's the one who tells me about Agora Training — that it's changed his life and that I should try it. He offers to help me with the fee.

Agora Training takes place over the course of 2 weekends. An Agora trainer focuses us on the conversations in our head: whether the conversations are positive or negative, constructive or destructive, directed to a goal or merely idle thoughts. I learn to consciously shift from negative notions to positive ones. To establish clear expectations regarding what it is I want in my life — rather than passively allowing things to unfold on their own.

At the end of the training, we're asked to write out our goals — to create a short-term vision and a long-term vision for our life. I remember writing down that I want to go back to school and get a GED, then go on to college and grad school, and someday become a psychotherapist. Even though I'm still not making enough money to properly feed myself and my sons, I feel there *must* be a way.

While at Agora Training I become friends with Dinah, a very sweet woman. I share with her that I'm in recovery from drug abuse. In turn, she shares with me that her adult daughter, Devorah, is using cocaine.

At Dinah's request, I soon meet Devorah. She's living in an abusive relationship with David, a used car dealer in Elmhurst. They have a son who is about a year old. Besides selling cars from a lot in Queens, David deals cocaine, and the 2 of them are heavy users. But I like Devorah, and we become good friends.

Thanksgiving, Christmas, and Easter

Sometime after Carlos enters rehab in late 1989, I go grocery shopping with Lukas and Johan. I don't have cash, but I do have a credit card. When we get to the checkout counter, though, my purchase is declined because I've reached my credit limit. My sons are scared and confused, since we have to leave a whole shopping cart of food at the store, returning home with nothing.

Not long afterward, Devorah comes by for a visit. When I open my refrigerator to get her some juice, she exclaims, "You have no food!"

Seeing how embarrassed and downcast I am, she then says, "Don't worry about it — we're going to Pathmark" (a local supermarket).

Devorah takes me there and spends $100 on food for me and my sons. It's been a long time since I've been able to buy that much food at one time (a full shopping cart back then). It feels like Thanksgiving, Christmas and Easter rolled into one!

I ask her, "You have so much money — what are you *doing?!*"

She answers, "Oh, no big deal. A little bit of kissy, kissy. Then f***, f***, f*** for a minute. I close my eyes, it's over and done with, and I have $100."

I'm like, "What are you talking about?"

She replies, "I'm working at a massage parlor."

My first thought is, *How gross!*

But then I have a moment of clarity: How much worse could it be than living like this? I've made many attempts to get work that would support myself and my sons — making pizzas and calzones, retail sales, real estate, cooking for Catholic priests in a seminary, driving for a car service, and cleaning homes. For awhile I had a 2nd job, delivering *The New York Daily News* to homes in Queens. I'd leave my house at 3 AM, return at 6 AM, get my sons ready for school, and then leave for my day job. (Sometimes little Lukas would help me deliver the paper on weekends.) But I *still* haven't been able to feed my sons properly.

I also think about the times when I was having such an excruciating toothache that I felt like hitting my head against the wall — but I couldn't afford to go to a dentist. And, all the years we've been living without health insurance, leaving me unable to take my sons or myself for medical checkups.

And now, I'm facing imminent eviction and the possibility of having to live with my boys in a New York City homeless shelter. At this moment, I realize that if there were ever a dilemma that calls for a *Plan B,* this is it.

I ask Devorah for the phone number of the place where she works. She hesitates, but then gives me the number of a friend of hers who knows people in the business.

Later, with a combination of resignation and trepidation, I call the number...

End of Book I

Gaetano Catelli is the author of *Behind Lesbia's Door: Her Slave-Girls' Shocking Revelations*, the true story of the woman at the center of the most notorious scandal of the ancient Roman Republic. (http://amzn.to/1bFoxgR)

www.ingramcontent.com/pod-product-compliance
Lightning Source LLC
Chambersburg PA
CBHW070957040426
42443CB00007B/547